Living Below with the Saints We Know

Living Below

with the Saints We Know

Strengthening Those Congregational Relationships

eagle

Guildford, Surrey

British Library Cataloguing in Publication Data. A catalogue record for this book is available from the British Library.

Published by Eagle, an imprint of Inter Publishing Service (IPS) Ltd, St Nicholas House, 14 The Mount, Guildford, Surrey GU2 5HN.

By the same author
Beyond Renewal – The Kingdom of God.
Word (UK) Ltd. 1990

Cover by Brian Pollard
Typeset at Eagle Publishing
Printed by Cox & Wyman

ISBN 0 86347 233 8

Acknowledgments

This book has been born out of the experiences of many people and I have been fortunate enough to be the recipient of their combined learning. No doubt this is one of the reasons why God has ordained that we should be in relationship with other Christians.

There are many people whom I wish to thank for their contributions to this book.

To my parents, now with the Lord, and home churches that nurtured me as a child and young person. To the many people from across the worldwide body of Christ whose friendship I appreciate and insights I have benefited from.

To those who have participated with me in the Te Atatu Bible Chapel eldership over the past years. For their encouragement to attempt this project and their key contribution to the pilgrimage that we have traversed together.

To my good friend and inveterate Coca Cola drinker, John Currie, for carefully reading and patiently correcting my primitive scientist grammar. I promise never again to commence a sentence with 'but'. May you even find the odd can of Coke in heaven for your labours!

To Hudson Salisbury who years ago started us on this pilgrimage of relationships with his emphasis and practical experience in this area.

To Gordon Miller and Lynn Goold for their helpful comments and encouragement.

To my many Maori friends whose relationship-base to living, aroha (love), open homes and generous hearts have been an inspiration to many of us.

To my wife Noeleen for her constant love, support, encouragement and numerous drinks sustaining me while producing the manuscript. She has been with me through the encouraging times and the difficult. Gratitude also is due to her and our children who, over the years, have had the love

and courage to confront me about the needs in my own relationships – not perfect, still growing.

The quotations and stories that have been used in this book
have been accumulated over many years. Some are my own.
Some have been slightly changed over time. Many have been
recorded with no knowledge of their origin. Where their origin is known, largely it has been acknowledged.

I dedicate this book to our children Glen, Sharon, Stephen
and Phillip, their wives Chrissy, Jo and Victoria and their
children. May they too discover the strength of committed
congregational relationships.

Finally my gratitude is expressed to God for his forgiveness, grace and strength, so abundantly showered on my
family and myself.

CONTENTS

INTRODUCTION

I listened with sadness as a friend told me of a recent church split. Of course it wasn't being touted as a church split. God had told them that it was time to 'plant a new congregation'.[1] 'This was the right moment.' It had been a 'mutual agreement' and they were going out with the 'blessing of the current leadership'. However I knew there had been agitation within the congregation for some months, maybe even years. The congregation had grown quickly and seen God's blessing. Some of the growth had come as people had left other churches where there had been tensions and struggles. Subsequently these churches had ironed out their problems and people who had left them gradually drifted back to their previous fellowships, but now it was a clear-cut division. Differences of opinion, of direction, of structure, these were the issues, not theology or church planting. Later the residing pastor was to use the word 'gutted' to me as he described what had happened.

> *Someone has said, 'Christians are so busy dividing that they have no time to multiply.'*

Such events are all too common. We can all recall vibrant, growing churches crippled by a split. Churches that were the 'in church', where it was the place to be. Hundreds, or maybe even thousands flocked to their services, but where are they today? They are either shells of their former selves or they have disappeared from the face of the earth. Where are the churches that have made a consistent impact for God for twenty years or more? Far too few examples can be given. Many other churches are in crisis – holding on by the skin of their teeth. Ministers and pastors are leaving the ministry worn out and destroyed, maybe never again to pastor God's people.

Why do big, apparently successful, churches suddenly collapse or decline over a number of years? Many valid reasons can be given. Maybe the charismatic leader left or demographic movements affected the congregation. Perhaps the leaders did not plan for the future or some moral issue surfaced. However we are all aware of another painful reason. One which has dogged humanity from the time of Cain and Abel. One which seems to spoil so much of human endeavour. I'm speaking of strained and broken relationships between people. Recent Australian research indicates that the most significant reason for people leaving parish ministry is conflict with local church leaders, 25 per cent left for this reason. In Baptist churches 70 per cent cited conflict with the congregation and/or its leaders as the key factor for leaving.[2]

No matter how well things are going there will always be someone complaining.

In the example given above, it was relationships between people that was the crux of the matter. Insufficient quality-time had been given to the relationships between pastoral staff and leadership. When things were progressing well and the congregation was buoyed along on the crest of the wave everything seemed sweet. There was enthusiasm, change, growth and a sense of expectancy. There was plenty to be done, new avenues to explore. However these can often mask underlying tensions between people. There is no time or apparent need to deal with these relationship issues when things are going well. We become lulled into a false sense of security. Then suddenly things can erupt. Issues that have been unresolved for years, hurts that have lain buried and disagreements swept under the carpet, can explode into the open and paralyse a leadership or congregation. People take sides, emotions become inflamed, telephones run hot and during congregational services you can cut the air with a knife. What has been built, suddenly collapses. Trust, that essential yet so fragile a commodity, is shattered, maybe never to be restored. Congregations split, the flock is scattered, bruised and hurt. Many never recover from such events and either drop out of church life or wander from place to place unable or unwilling to put their roots down again. Others recover but the process is slow and painful.

Such events break the heart of God, mock the cross of Jesus and dishonour the ministry of the Holy Spirit.

Does it honour God if congregations grow quickly only to fracture and divide later?

The title for this book comes from the saying – 'Living above with the saints we love, that will be glory. Living below with the saints we know – that's another story.' It is about relationships in churches. It is insights gleaned over twenty-five years of involvement in congregational life. Years that have included change, controversy and growth. Maybe this topic is a lot less glamorous than many others that are written about, but it is my conviction that this topic is one of the highest priorities in God's eyes.

We need to address some issues. Does it honour God if congregations grow quickly only to fracture and divide later? Maybe in our keenness to evangelise, we place too great an emphasis on church growth or church planting and too little on our relationships together. Is our Christianity more orientated towards 'doing' than 'being'? After all, as someone has said, God created 'human beings' not 'human doings'. With all the good that has come out of the Pentecostal wing of the Church, it is still the most divided stream of the worldwide Church. How has an embracing of the work of the Holy Spirit contributed to so much division?

Many books are written on marriage and family, and justifiably so, as this is the foundation of our society. However not so many are written about relationships with others in general congregational life, in small groups or in leadership teams.

It is with a sense of urgency that I write on this subject. Urgency, because of the extent of the problem. It has been my sad portion to minister in many churches and talk to many pastors and leadership teams from all denominational backgrounds who are struggling with tense relationships in their congregation or at leadership level. Over the past years one third of the congregations around the world that I have been involved with have either experienced a recent split in the congregation or there were serious relationship difficulties within the leadership team.

> ***The basic cause of most inharmonious relationships
> is the tendency to impose our values on other people.***

Whichever the case, the congregations had been immobilised. As I ask them about how much time they have spent developing relationships within the congregation or leadership team, without exception they say that they have not emphasised these areas of Christian life. Young people I talk to tell me that they seldom, if ever, hear any teaching on the subject of how to get on with their brothers and sisters in Christ within their congregation, their small group or their team that oversees some area of congregational activities.

In a previous book[3] I outlined some of the events that God took our congregation through during charismatic renewal. I now regret that the first chapter of that book did not deal with relationships. Long before we experienced renewal through the charismatic movement, God had led us to explore deeper relationships within leadership and within the congregation. We had formed small groups in 1970, explored greater intimacy at leadership level and run 'Body Life' services where personal needs were expressed, ministered to and prayed for. It was from that base of closer relationships within the congregation that so many changes were able to be effected, changes that have often split other churches. It was not a strategy that we developed, it was simply through the goodness of God that this happened. God built into our leaders and congregation a very firm and secure foundation on which many other things would be built. We have been privileged to experience very little tension in leadership and in thirty years, by the grace of God, have never gone through a church split. During this time major changes have been faced, worked through and embraced. Such issues have involved the ministry of the Holy Spirit, social concern, restructuring of leadership (several times), congregational services and the role of women. Coming from a conservative evangelical background these have not been easy changes to implement. We are far from perfect. There have been tense times where personal issues have needed to be addressed and worked through. Relationships have been strained. People have left the congregation for a variety of reasons. We have seen marriage breakups and encountered sad and very difficult situations that have had to be faced. However, underneath, there has been a strong desire to work these through on the basis of our commitment to Jesus Christ and to each other. We are grateful for the foundation of closer relationships that God has given us. It is a foundation that takes time to establish and we constantly have to return to it, strengthen it, remind each other of it and teach on it.

There is also a strong sense of reluctance to write on the topic of relationships. Reluctance because of one's own weakness and failings in this area and because of the needs within one's own congregation. I am no more qualified, probably less than most, to raise this topic. I do it because of its centrality to our Christian faith and the fact that most of the world's problems – some would say all – result from broken relationships between people and God, and people themselves. Nothing is perfect in congregational life, although sometimes it seems that way when books are written. The congregation that has nurtured my family and myself over the last twenty-five years is just like any other – full of people. When we have people we have problems. It is often out of the heartache that we hear the still small voice of God and discover his abiding principles.

> *God has given us other Christians as a test of our love.*

In this book we will look at how self-centredness, pride and competition, such valued attitudes within our society, actually contribute so much towards breakdown in relationships. We will discover that these problems are as old as sin itself and Scripture has answers for them. We will see that God places a high priority on the quality of our relationships together and that he has an incredible goal for us in this area – relationships between Christians are to mirror the relationship between the members of the Trinity. In fact the biblical view of Christian life is a corporate view rather than an individual one – all the more reason to address this important matter. Among other things, we will look at ways in which teams can function more effectively together and discuss the part our physical resources play in our relationships together.

This book has been written with group interaction in mind. It is anticipated that cell groups, leadership teams and people in other types of groups will benefit by working together through the questions in the Study Guide.

Much of what is shared here has come from personal reflection, discussion with many others across the body of Christ and out of personal, sometimes bitter experience. There is still much to be learned and much more to be applied. I am only too well aware of this. I share these insights with the humble expectation that God will minister to others within his body.

1

THE PASSION OF JESUS

It was evening in a room above a busy street in Jerusalem.
The last few days had been climactic. There was the entrance
by donkey into the city. It seemed as if the whole city had
turned out. Crowds – Cheering – Palm leaves – Shouting –
Excitement – Joy – Coats strewn on the road. Then there was
the fig tree on the road from Bethany – withered overnight –
quite incredible! There followed those events in the temple,
that whip of cords, the eyes of the money changers as their
tables overturned – fear, surprise, anger – the little children
scrambling to pick up the coins. Then the sullen, surly religious leaders whose demanding interrogations were met
only by penetrating questions from the Master. There was
the meal, the strange use of bread and wine – something to
do with 'not repeating it until he came into his kingdom'.

He always seemed to be talking about that kingdom – was
this the time he would establish it?

There was John, whispering to the Master. Peter, forcefully
declaring his loyalty. Judas, darting out to buy food – hesi-
tant, suspicious-looking. Then there were those wise words
the Master spoke, so many of them. He seemed to be more
earnest, intense, forward-looking, as if some momentous
event lay ahead. Those around were very attentive, holding
onto every word, obviously savouring the event and occasionally interjecting with a question for clarification.

Then, suddenly, the Master stops speaking. He lifts his
eyes heavenward and begins to pray to his Father. There is

an abruptness about this action. One moment he is scanning
the faces of those around him as he shares truths from the
heart of his Father, the next almost oblivious of them, pour-
ing out his heart in prayer. He seems totally detached from
those around, almost as if they do not exist. They are trans-
fixed. It is the outpouring of the Master's heart that holds
their attention. They had heard him pray before but never
like this. The Master is totally taken up with what he is praying.

This is a prayer of deep intimacy and great intensity.

'Father . . . Father . . . Father . . .' he prays. This is a prayer of
deep intimacy and great intensity. A prayer of fervour and
urgency. The prayer of a person who knows his mission on
earth is nearly complete. 'Father you are in me and I am in
you, may they be in us so that the world will believe that you
sent me.' 'Father may they be one as we are one.' 'Father may
they be brought to complete unity.' 'Father may the love you
have for me be in them' (Jn 17).

It pours out of the Master. Never before in the three-and-a-
half years that he has been with them have his disciples
heard him pray like this. Passion, that's what it is – passion.
They fasten their eyes on him.

Relationships – the passion of Jesus

Do you want to know what is on a person's heart? Listen to
them pray – really pray. Jesus' prayer (Jn 17) exudes love,
devotion and unity between the Father and Son.

This prayer is a prayer of passion. This is what has been on
the Master's heart. This is why he has been sent. This is the
goal he has had before him. Here we see right into the very
purposes of the Trinity.

What is this passion? Is it a passion for evangelism? No! Is
it a passion for planting churches or church growth? No! Is
it a passion for revival? No! In one word it is a passion for
UNITY. Unity among his people! Harmonious relationships,
that is what is really on the heart of God.

This prayer just breathes relationship, fellowship, intimacy.

The words tumble over each other – I, you, me, them, they, your, mine, we, us. One hundred and sixty-eight pronouns in twenty-six verses. Probably nowhere in Scripture are so many pronouns linked together – over six per verse. This prayer just breathes relationship, fellowship, intimacy.

In this chapter Christ links himself to the Father as many times as he links us to either the Father or Son. Forty-two times the Father and Son are linked together – you/me, I/you, us. Forty-two times we are linked to either the Father and/or Son – I/you/those, they/yours, you/them/me, I/them, they/you/me.

Consider some of these statements and notice the pronouns;

- '. . . glorify YOUR Son that YOUR Son may glorify YOU' (v 1)
- 'I have brought YOU glory on earth by completing the work YOU gave ME' (v 4)
- 'I have revealed YOU to those whom YOU gave ME . . . THEY were YOURS; YOU gave THEM to ME' (v 6)
- '. . . everything YOU have given ME comes from YOU' (v 7)
- 'I gave THEM the words YOU gave ME' (v 8)
- 'THEY knew with certainty that I came from YOU' (v 9)
- 'All I have is YOURS, and all YOU have is MINE' (v 10)
- '. . . that THEY may be one as WE are one' (vv 11, 22)
- 'YOU are in ME and I am in YOU' (v 21)
- ' . . . may THEY also be one in US' (v 21)
- 'I in THEM and YOU in ME' (v 23)
- 'May THEY be brought to complete unity' (v 23)

Here we catch a glimpse of that astonishing relationship between Father and Son. This prayer reflects the intimacy of the Trinity – 'you are in me and I am in you' (v 21). Here we see Christ's goal for human relationships, the possibility of his followers enjoying the same quality of relationship both with each other and with the Father and himself. This is his passion and the central focus of this prayer.

Father, Son and Spirit always work together out of a glorious co-operative, united relationship.

Try to visualise the unity and intimacy of relationship between Father, Son and Spirit. Words such as love, devotion, loyalty, affection, support, integrity, co-operation, harmony, commitment, honour, trust, transparency, interdependence, joy, security and unity barely begin to scratch the surface of this glorious relationship.

Father, Son and Spirit always work together out of a glorious co-operative, united relationship.

- We see this in creation – God said 'let **us** make man in our image' (Gen 1:26).
- We see this in the life of **Jesus** – as he walked this life in obedience to the will of the **Father** (Jn 8:29) empowered by the indwelling **Holy Spirit** (Lk 4:18).
- We see this in redemption – '**Christ** through the eternal **Spirit** offered himself' (Heb 9:14), while '**God** [Father] was in Christ, reconciling the world unto himself' (2 Cor 5:19 AV).
- We see this in the giving of the Holy Spirit – '**I** [Christ] will ask the **Father,** and he will give you . . . the **Spirit**' (Jn 14:16).
- We see this in our salvation – '**He** [Father] saved us through the washing of rebirth and renewal by the **Holy Spirit**, whom he poured out on us generously through **Jesus Christ** our Saviour, so that, having been justified by his grace, we might become heirs having the hope of eternal life' (Tit 3:5–7).
- We see this in the giving of the gifts – 'There are different kinds of gifts, but the same **Spirit** . . . different kinds of service, but the same **Lord** . . . different kinds of working, but the same **God** [Father]' (1 Cor 12:4).
- We see this in the life of the Christian – strengthened 'with power through his **Spirit** in your inner being . . .' **Christ** dwelling in your hearts by faith . . . filled with all the fulness of **God** [Father] (Eph 3:16–19).
- We see this in the Church – 'Make every effort to keep

the unity of the Spirit . . . There is one body and one **Spirit** . . . one **Lord** . . . one God and **Father**' (Eph 4:3–6).
- We see it in the 'sonship' that Christians have been brought into – 'Because you are sons, **God** [Father] sent the **Spirit** of his **Son** into our hearts, the Spirit who calls out, "*Abba*, Father"' (Gal 4:6).
- We see this in the bringing together of Jew and Gentile – '**He** [Christ] came and preached peace to you who were far away and peace to those who were near. For through him we both have access to the **Father** by one **Spirit**' (Eph 2:18).
- We see it in the 'grace' – 'May the grace of the **Lord Jesus Christ**, and the love of **God** [Father], and the fellowship of the **Holy Spirit** be with you all' (2 Cor 13:14).
- We see this in heaven – the **Father** is on the throne, the **Son** saying 'Behold, I am coming soon! My reward is with me.' The **Spirit** bidding us to 'Come' (Rev 22).

This unity and co-operation between Father, Son and Spirit is seen in the first chapter of the Book and in the last. Harmony, interdependence and unity in relationships between the members of the Trinity.

This relationship between Father and Son is the example for all Christian relationships.

This intimate relationship on earth between Father and Son was the outworking of the will of God in the life of Jesus. It was a continuation of the intimacy of eternity, now being observed on earth. It was one of the evidences of the kingdom of God seen in the life of Jesus.

There is more. This relationship between Father and Son is the example for all Christian relationships. This is the standard, it is the yardstick, anything else is second-rate. This is the model for Christian marriage and family. This is the model for relationships within and between local congregations. This is the model for home-groups, church committees, youth ministry and leadership teams. This is the example for the worldwide body of Christ. This is the maturity that God has in store for his people (Eph 4:13), oneness exemplified by that between Father and Son – 'that they may be one as we are one' (Jn 17:22).

In this relationship between Father and Son we have a picture of mutual interdependence. Jesus says 'You are in me and I am in you' (Jn 17:21). He is completely identified with his Father – 'Your interests are my interests, your goals are my goals. I am dependent on you, you are dependent on me. I know what you want me to do and I'll do what you want me to do.'

This is the passion of Jesus. He desires that the respect, co-operation, interdependence and depth of relationship enjoyed by himself and his Father, might be ours. We with him and with each other.

> *Humanity stands alone over all of creation in this one unique purpose – fellowship with the Maker.*

Relationships – the goal of creation

This prayer of Jesus spans the whole of eternity. It is birthed in eternity past – 'you loved me before the creation of the world' (v 24), is outworked in time – 'I pray for those you have given me' (v 9), 'I pray for those who will believe in me' (v 20) and looks towards eternity future – 'I want those you have given me to be with me where I am' (v 24).

Consider God's purpose in creating people. The biblical record indicates that God created humanity in order that he might enjoy relationship with people. We are created uniquely in his image to voluntarily enjoy fellowship with him, to stand alone over all of creation in this one unique purpose – fellowship with the Maker. Humanity is remarkably different from the rest of the material universe or other created spirit beings. We are created to share in the fellowship of the Trinity. Picture the joy of the Godhead as they anticipated this event. Imagine the surprise of the angelic hosts or the evil scheming of the demonic hosts as they watched what was happening. 'Let us make people in our image, let us walk with them in the garden, let us enjoy their fellowship and they ours.' Such were the purposes of God.

Imagine then the hurt that sin and the fall brought to God. Let us try to see this from God's point of view. So often we look at things only from our human viewpoint. What's in it for me? We appeal to selfish interests. My salvation, my healing, my deliverance, my security, my peace, my joy – self-centred Christianity.

God comes in the cool of the evening to the garden for fellowship with humanity and finds Adam and Eve afraid and hiding. Had the Son ever hidden from the Father or the Spirit from the Son? Had the Spirit ever been afraid of the Father or the Father of the Son? How absurd!

God calls to Adam, 'Where are you?' This sounds like the cry of a parent whose child has wandered away from the security of the family, or of a mother desperately seeking a lost infant. Can you hear the hurt, the sorrow, the ache in the Father's heart? Consider this further question, 'What have you done?' Understand the sorrow, the surprise, the hurt and dismay. Why are you hiding? I did not create you for this! Fractured relationships – that is at the centre of these two painful questions wrenched from the heart of God.

Sense the heart of God at the second recorded sin as he comes to Cain after he had killed his brother in a fit of jealousy. Hear these two questions again, 'Where is your brother?' 'What have you done?' Again God comes to humanity, his response registers consternation and dismay.

Sin shatters relationships, destroys intimacy, annihilates trust and wrecks unity.

'Where are you?' 'What have you done?' 'Where is your brother?' 'What have you done?' What words can possibly describe how God felt on these occasions? Agony? Distress? Anguish? Heartbreak? Pain? Grief? Hurt? No doubt all this and more. The dream had been destroyed, the relationship severed. Sin had divided; it always divides. It had divided God from people in the garden. It had divided brother from brother outside the garden. How absolute was the breakdown of that relationship – murder. No possible hope of reconciliation. Sin shatters relationships, destroys intimacy, annihilates trust and wrecks unity.

Parents have great joy when they see their children in unity, but great hurt where there is division and tension. David said, 'How good and pleasant it is when brothers live together in unity' (Ps 133:1) and he ought to know after all that his family went through – incest, murder and insurrection.

Can we feel the ache in God's heart over the succeeding centuries, or hear his agonising cry 'What have you done?' as humans inflict hurt, pain, misery and death on their own kind. The Crusades. Hitler, the Jews and the gas chambers. Famine in Africa. Vietnam. The abused children in homes and in play centres – two areas where there should be greatest security. The 150,000 babies aborted every day around this planet. The broken marriages and splintered families. The division in his body today, the competitiveness, church splits, hostility and empire building. Or what about the things we say, think and do to each other in our congregations?

'Where are you?' 'What have you done?' Hear the heart of God as he surveys the wreckage of broken human relationships strewn over this planet. 'I didn't create you for this. You were created for fellowship, for intimacy, for security and for joy. What have you done?'

Does God grieve today over broken human relationships?

We need to feel something of the heart of the Father if we are to fully understand the passion of Jesus as seen in John 17. We must grasp God's initial desires and plans for humanity if we are to enter into an understanding of this Passover prayer prayed above those busy Jerusalem streets. This is where this prayer comes from, birthed in eternity past, to be outworked in time and heading for eternity ijn the future.

Does God grieve today over broken human relationships? Are we going too far, is imagination running riot to say that God feels deeply over anything that mars, breaks, spoils or destroys relationships? That my broken relationships cause an ache in the heart of God? Well, the Holy Spirit is grieved (he sorrows, has distress, is pained) today (Eph 4:30). What is it that grieves the Spirit today? Anger, stealing, unwholesome words, bitterness, rage, brawling, slander and malice are the relationship words that are the context to this verse. These attitudes and actions are what grieves the Holy Spirit today. Don't those seem very much like the same attitudes that led to that first murder and caused God's heartbroken cry of 'What have you done?' Broken human relationships still cause grief to God today.

Relationships – their restoration

Why did Jesus come to this planet? Torn from the side of his Father to tread the dusty paths of Palestine that led him to the cross. Did he see the ache and pain in the Father's heart over broken human relationships? Did he not come to earth to make it possible for relationship to be restored; restored between God and people and between people themselves? Surely this is the core of the gospel message. He saw something in the Father's heart, he felt the ache and sensed the sorrow.

'I will go Father,' and he laid everything down for it.

The cost of restoration

And the cost of this restoration of relationships for Jesus? Incredible! Ponder these steps:

The frailty of becoming a human baby.
The shame of illegitimacy.
The terror of being a refugee.
The experience of an oppressive occupying power.
The learning of a trade.
The grief at the loss of an earthly father.
The direct confrontation with Satan.
The hunger from fasting.
The disappointment of unbelief in his home town.

The humility of washing dusty feet.
The weariness of constant ministry.
The frustration with his disciples.
The misappropriation of money by a follower.
The scorn and criticism as he:
>   befriended prostitutes
>   chose terrorists as disciples
>   had meals with corrupt businessmen
>   cared for lepers
>   did good on the Sabbath
>   ministered to non-Jews.

The hatred and opposition of the religious leaders.
The fickle nature of the masses.
The ingratitude of so many he ministered to.
The treachery of the betrayal by Judas.
The agony in the garden.
The temptation to avoid the cross.
The loneliness as his followers desert him.
The heartbreak of denial by his key leader.
The injustice of an illegal trial.
The lies and slander in front of Pilate.
The mockery of Herod.
The manipulation of the mob at his trial.
The physical pain as hair was pulled from his face.
The agony of the beating.
The disgrace of human spittle trickling down his face.
The anguish and shame of crucifixion.
The curses of the soldiers.
The insults of the onlookers.
The gloating of his enemies.
The revulsion of being made sin.
The horror of death.
The forsaking by his Father – the shattering of the Trinity.
The permanent alteration to the Trinity now – Christ has a
>   resurrected body in heaven.

Almost all of the above occurrences in the life of Christ are
the result of sin and what it produces in human relation-

ships. Grief, disappointment, scorn, hatred, ingratitude, loneliness, lies, mockery, insults, curses and more – all describing human relationships. While on this earth Jesus endured all the common experiences of broken human relationships. Maybe we can understand a bit more when we read '[he] made himself nothing, taking the very nature of a servant, being made in human likeness. And being found in appearance as a man, he humbled himself and became obedient to death' (Phil 2:7–8).

The price we pay for something gives us an idea of its value. What price did God pay for restoration of relationships?

On the cross there was wrung from his lips the cry 'My God, my God why have you forsaken me?' There were no open heavens here. No dove descending. No voice of commendation. No crowd applauding. Only the silence of eternity punctuated by the rumble of earthquake, the tearing of temple veil and an eerie midday darkness. The fellowship, the intimacy, the love, the devotion, the security, the unity between Father and Son from all eternity replaced by the emptiness, desolation and horror of a shattered relationship.

Was the relationship of the Trinity shattered so that the relationship between God and humanity could be restored? Is this the cost for restoration of relationship between God and people? The price we pay for something gives us an idea of its value. What price did God pay for restoration of relationships? The ultimate price, therefore relationships are of the ultimate value. Yet we throw them away, for a cheap shot, a critical spirit, the jabs and jibes we level at those we disagree with, the proud heart which refuses to reconcile with a brother or sister, the talk that goes on behind another's back, the grudges that we bear, the unforgiveness that we harbour in our lives, the resentments that smoulder and grow into bitterness, the unchecked information that we spread about a member of our fellowship, the competitiveness between church leaders. We grieve the Spirit. Maybe God is saying to us, 'Where are you? Where is your brother, your sister? What have you done?' Is there something spoiling God's intention for you? For your congregation?

Christ's passion, our passion?

These then are the truths that underpin the prayer of Jesus on that Passover night. The goal of creation, the ache of the Father's heart, the restoration of God's purposes. These realities form the backdrop to this prayer. This is where the prayer generates its passion.

Christ has no passion for many of our flashy programmes. He has no passion for our buildings and our church structures. He has no passion for our denominational or theological distinctiveness. He has no passion for our worldwide end-time plans. He has one undying passion – it is for our unity. 'Father may they be one as we are one' – here is where we see his passion.

Our human minds protest. Such relationships between human beings are impractical, unrealistic and totally impossible. Human nature will never change to such a degree. Pause a minute. Are not many of God's ideals for us seemingly beyond us? How can we be holy as he is holy (1 Pet 1:15–16)? Or what about doing the things that he has done and even greater than these (Jn 14:12)?

God's longings for us are always modelled and based on the example of his Son. It is his intention that we should be like Jesus. This is the goal for which we are created. It is not an unattainable ideal – one day God is going to have us like his Son. Until then we press towards this goal (Phil 3:7–14).

It was to establish relationships like those enjoyed within the Trinity that Jesus came to earth. He prayed for it. He died for it. He sent the Holy Spirit for it. He is interceding for it now. He is coming back for it. Is such unity in relationships too much to hope for? Yes, it is, if we did not have John chapter seventeen in our Bibles!

> ***God's love is redemptive. People's love is
> self-serving. Satan's 'love' is destructive.***

Observe the results of such relationship – authority (v 2),

insight (revelation) (v 6), knowledge and faith (v 8), protection and identity ('given a name') (v 11), joy (v 13), mission ('they were sent') (v 18), set apart for God's special purpose (sanctification) (v 19), unity and glory (v 21), witness (the world will know the Father sent Christ and loves us) (v 23), revelation of the Father's love in us (v 26). What a marvellous set of outcomes flow from such relationships. Outcomes that were seen to the full in the life of Jesus and are the desires of the Father and Son for us now. There is not much missing from this list; they embrace most of the longings of our redeemed hearts.

What is our vision and what are we going to settle for? All too often we allow ourselves to be moulded by our cultural norms and expectations. We may live in a very independent, individualistic culture but that does not make it right. How big is our vision? Many seem to live with narrow tunnel-vision in self-centred congregational or denominational worlds. Christ's vision was so broad. Can we embrace John 17 as our *modus operandi*?

> *Change in attitudes must always precede change in practice. Before seeds can grow and multiply they have to be planted.*

This 'oneness' has God as both its source and its example. In practice it may be difficult to achieve the level of relationships that Jesus prayed for, but it must be our goal. Change in attitudes must always precede change in practice. Before seeds can grow and multiply they have to be planted.

We flock to seminars on evangelism, church growth, worship, signs and wonders and counselling, but what about seminars on unity? Seminars on unity just aren't offered. Nobody would attend! Surely this indicates we are running to our own agendas and not God's agenda. Is it because we have not seen this passion and priority of Jesus? So often those of us in pastoral ministry find it easier to shy away from events that foster unity. We feel threatened, uncomfortable, and defensive.

We need to sense the heart of Jesus on this matter and

weep at the mess we have made of the body of Christ. All too often we have legitimised independence, sanctified the sinful nature and worshipped at the shrine of our cultural values.

Are we going to finish up with an ever-increasing range of congregations catering for what we see are 'the needs of special groups of people'? Will this demonstrate the unity that Christ yearns for or will it just prove to the world that the church is as fractured as they are?

God has bridged the largest gap imaginable – that between himself and fallen people. All other divides can now be bridged – cultural, age, gender, socio-economic. God intends that his people demonstrate this, not only to a watching world but also to the spiritual powers. 'His intent was that now, through the church, the manifold wisdom of God should be made known to the rulers and authorities in the heavenly realms' (Eph 3:10). What is God's wisdom? Infinite variety in perfect harmony – that is God's wisdom and that is God's intention for his people. We had better make sure that the next time we cause a church split the reason for the split is of greater importance than what motivated this passion of Jesus.

We must no longer filter the John 17 prayer of Jesus through our own understanding, goals or past experiences of relationships. Let us see it for what it is, the PASSION OF JESUS for deep relationships between his people.

This passion for quality relationships between his people is what we will be turning our attention to in the following chapters.

2

GOD'S PRIORITY: OUR PRIORITY?

I was talking to Peter[1] a young man who had just taken on the leadership of a major para-church organisation in our city.

'Our church has just been through a massive split,' he said sadly. 'It was terrible. Jane[2] and I are really hurting, we have so little emotional energy left. We have only just hung in there. We wanted to leave many times.'

'Unfortunately you are not alone in this,' I replied gently, 'I have talked to many like yourselves who have experienced similar circumstances.'

'Some of our best friends have left,' he continued. 'Now we seldom see them. It's affected our families and there has been a three-way split in the fellowship – one third has left to form a new congregation, one third has left and are not going to any church and one third has remained.'

Peter's church had come from a conservative evangelical background. Over the previous seven years the pastor had been trying to bring the congregation into a greater experience and appreciation of the gifts of the Spirit.

'There had been a lot of emphasis on the ministry of the Holy Spirit and developing of gifts,' Peter explained. 'My wife and I were very committed to this teaching and we had enthusiastically embraced this new emphasis. It was exciting to see the church growing rapidly.'

'How much time did the pastor spend on teaching about relationships within the congregation over this time?' I asked.

Peter thought for a minute.

'Almost none,' he replied.

Almost none in seven years of pastoral ministry in a large city church! Yet the New Testament writers spend so much time on this area. Is it any wonder that when the pressure comes on there is a split in the congregation. Anyway, what does it prove if the gifts operate but the church splits? Does it not indicate that we are just like the world – they cannot get on with people when they disagree, neither can we. The saddest thing is that the members of Peter's congregation probably agreed on 99.5 per cent of things pertaining to their church life and practice but split over the 0.5 per cent – how ridiculous!

> *Thirty per cent of the content of the epistles deals*
> *with relationships, while only three per cent*
> *deals with gifts of the Spirit.*

God's priority – relationships

Consider the high priority God places on our relationships together:

a) Of the ten commandments, the first four have to do with relationship with God, the last six have to do with relationships between people.

b) It is estimated that 44 per cent of the content of the epistles has to do with relationships – how Christians get on together. If the writers of the epistles spent this much time addressing relationships in the first-century churches, are the twentieth-century churches now mature enough to bypass these issues?

c) The writers of the epistles spend ten times more time talking about relationships than talking about spiritual gifts. Does the average charismatic or Pentecostal pastor maintain the same ratio?

d) The Bible gives clear instructions about relationships:
   - In family – husbands to wives, wives to husbands, children to parents, parents to children
   - In work – employee to employer, employer to employee
   - In the congregation – leaders to those in the congregation, those in the congregation towards leaders, congregational members towards other congregational members
   - In society – towards governments, towards our enemies, towards others in society.

e) We see that relationships between people in the first-century church (Acts 2:42–47) embraced the:
   - Social dimension – they had fellowship, met together
   - Intellectual dimension – devoted themselves to the apostles' teaching
   - Material dimension – had things in common, shared possessions
   - Spiritual dimension – praised and worshipped God
   - Emotional dimension – enjoyed the favour of all people
   - Cultural dimension – people from many language and culture groups came together.

There is great comfort in being with someone where
you do not have to weigh thoughts
or measure words.

f) We frequently read the word 'together' in the New Testament. Here are some of the things Christians are encouraged to do together – agree, assemble, be refreshed, bring, build, be called, cleave, come, be comforted, consult, follow, be fitted, gather, grow, be joined, live, knit, be planted, meet, run, sow, strive, struggle, work, sing.

g) A further relationship word is the Greek word *allelon* normally translated 'one another'. This word occurs fifty-nine times as part of a specific command.[3] We are encouraged to – love another, be devoted to one another, accept one another, have concern for one another, carry one another's burdens, forgive one another, submit to one another, pray for one another, confess sins to one another, etc.

How often have we wrestled with the practical outworking of these 'one another' commands? These are not just a set of nice ideas. What do they mean in practice? How do we apply these in the twentieth century? It is not good enough to say that the Holy Spirit will work these out in our lives. As God works in us – instructing us, showing us his priorities – we need to work this out (Phil 2:12–13). This working out, says Paul, is in terms of obedience. Would it not have been wiser for the pastor of Peter's church to have spent time teaching on the practical outworking of some of these commands, rather than spending so much time preaching on the gifts of the Spirit? In fact 1 Corinthians 13:1–3 indicates that impressive gifts can be used (tongues, prophecy, fathoming mysteries, knowledge and faith), social action may occur (giving possessions to the poor) and the ultimate self-sacrifice be made (giving one's body to be burned) but none of these have any value whatsoever if they do not function out of love.

What are the qualities of love? 1 Corinthians 13:4–7 tells us that love is patience, kindness, it does not boast, is not rude, is not self-seeking. All these are relationship responses to those around us. Love is simply being committed to the highest good of another.

It is so distressing to see so-called mature Christians running around displaying spiritual gifts, seeking after the next prophetic word from the latest 'anointed prophet', when their relationships in marriage, family or with congregational members are prickly or, even worse, falling apart. This does not honour the ministry of the Spirit. Let's get real folks!

We will be returning again to some of these 'one

another' statements in the following two chapters.

'Love is to the heart what the summer's sun is to the
farmer's harvest. It brings to harvest all
the loveliest flowers of the soul.'
Billy Graham

h) The most often repeated command in the New
Testament is 'Love one another'. Sixteen times it is
recorded in the New Testament.[4] The Holy Spirit sees
fit to repeat this command more often than other commandments such as to repent, or pray for each other.
Surely it gives us some indication as to what is really
on God's heart. Of course praying for each other and
repentance are also important. However we need to
have God's priority.

i) The words most often associated with the old nature or
the fruit of the Spirit are words describing relationships. These attitudes and actions are the fruit of the
root.

The old nature:

The acts of the sinful nature are obvious: sexual
immorality, impurity and debauchery; idolatry and
witchcraft; hatred, discord, jealousy, fits of rage, selfish
ambition, dissensions, factions and envy; drunkenness, orgies, and the like. I warn you, as I did before,
that those who live like this will not inherit the kingdom of God.

(Gal 5:19–21)

Hatred, discord, jealousy, fits of rage, selfish ambition,
dissensions, factions and envy, all speak of relationship problems between people.

The fruit of the Spirit:

But the fruit of the Spirit is love, joy, peace, patience,
kindness, goodness, faithfulness, gentleness and self-

control. Against such things there is no law. Those who belong to Christ Jesus have crucified the sinful nature with its passions and desires. Since we live by the Spirit, let us keep in step with the Spirit. Let us not become conceited, provoking and envying each other.
(Gal 5:22–26)

Love, joy, peace, patience, kindness, goodness, faithfulness, gentleness and self-control, all of these qualities reflect the way we relate to other people.
The ministry of the Spirit is both hindered by spoiled human relationships and enhanced by healthy ones

j)   Many of the portions in the New Testament where instructions about the ministry of the Spirit are outlined are surrounded by verses about relationships:
   • Instruction on the filling of the Spirit (Eph 5), is in the context of relationships.
   • Instruction on grieving the Spirit (Eph 4:22–32), is in the context of relationships.
   • Instruction on the leading of the Spirit (Gal 5:13–23), is in the context of relationships.
   • Instruction on the gifts of the Holy Spirit (Rom 12; 1 Cor 12, Eph 4), is in the context of relationships.
   • Instruction on the baptism of the Spirit (1 Cor 12:13), is in the context of relationships. In fact this is the main reason for the baptism of the Spirit. Jews or Greeks, slave or free – two of the huge relationship divisions of the New Testament church – were baptised into the one body. Clearly the Holy Spirit is saying that this baptism enables these groups to get on together.
One has to assume that the ministry of the Spirit is both hindered by spoiled human relationships and enhanced by healthy relationships between the people of God. Why is it that the Pentecostal stream of the Church, which has majored so much on the ministry of the Holy Spirit, has become the most divided stream in

all of church history! I do not say this so we can take a pot shot at Pentecostals. Many of them are my friends and God has greatly blessed this stream of the Church. It in turn has been a great blessing to other sectors of the body of Christ. Where fruit and gifts combine together we have enormous strength and many Pentecostal groups have been able to merge these effectively.

k) The greatest commandments are to 'love God and love our neighbour'. This emphasises our relationship with God and our relationships with others. All of the law is fulfilled if we obey this commandment.

Most of humanity's conflicts are not struggles between right and wrong, but between people who are either too proud or too powerful.

l) The New Testament indicates that as this age comes to a close, human relationships are going to steadily get worse.

But mark this: There will be terrible times in the last days. People will be lovers of themselves, lovers of money, boastful, proud, abusive, disobedient to their parents, ungrateful, unholy, without love, unforgiving, slanderous, without self-control, brutal, not lovers of the good, treacherous, rash, conceited, lovers of pleasure rather than lovers of God.

(2 Tim 3:1–4)

What a picture of much of twentieth-century society – self-centred humanity. Notice the relationship words – boastful, proud, abusive, disobedient to their parents, ungrateful, brutal, treacherous.

Most, maybe all, problems in society and within the church ultimately come back to relationship problems and tensions between people.

As we reflect on all of the above points it becomes patently obvious that God places a great emphasis on the way we Christians get on together (or should be getting on together!). The question has to be asked, 'Do we view these issues in the same light as God does?' Have we seen this area of Christian life as a priority? If Peter's church is any indication, then perhaps many of us have missed this emphasis.

All too often churches fall prey to the human success syndrome: bigger, better, brighter. Have we fallen prey to an over-emphasis on church growth, church planting, numbers, buildings, finances? These all have a legitimate place, but far too often those of us in church leadership measure success in these terms only. All of these success criteria are non-biblical criteria. How does God view 'success'? Maybe God uses different criteria to measure it. As I try to understand the heart of Jesus from his prayer in John 17, I have been coming to the conclusion God's view of 'success' is very different from ours. If it is, then surely we need to carefully reconsider our criteria.

'Is God's priority our priority?'

KEEP IT UP – SORT IT OUT!

There is a story told about some people who visited hell. It was nothing like what they thought it might be. They were taken into a large banquet room where they saw tables laden with all kinds of sumptuous food. Sitting around the tables were hundreds and hundreds of people, each with a knife and fork in their hands. However the visitors noticed something strange. The people had arms that would not bend at the elbows. The visitors watched in horror as they saw those around the tables feverishly trying to shovel the food into their mouths using their long stiff arms and having almost no success. There were groans and cries of consternation as much of the food found its way onto the floor. Fights regularly broke out among those around the tables trying to stuff their mouths with the food.

The visitors were then taken into heaven and were surprised to see almost the same scene. The tables were laden with the same sumptuous food, hundreds sitting with arms fixed at the elbows. However the scene was different. There was no fighting and each person was enjoying eating food from the laden tables. The difference? In heaven they were feeding each other.

God's intention has always been that human beings should live interdependently and co-operatively. He created us to relate socially. In Genesis we read that God said, 'It is not good for the man to be alone' (Gen 2:18), so he created Eve as a companion for Adam. Relationships – their establishment and development – are at the centre of God's intentions for humanity. The family was established by God as a structure for the development of relationships and the Church was instituted for the enrichment of relationships between Christians. It is only through relationships that we will come to maturity in Christ – we could never become like Christ living on an island by ourselves. The Spirit of God gives gifts to people to mature others around about and these gifts function as we come into relationships with others. Gifts of God's Spirit function through relationships and for relationships.

> **'When a thorn pierces the foot, the whole body must bend over to pull it out.'**
> **Zulu proverb**

It was pointed out in the previous chapter that the writers of the New Testament are at pains to emphasise relationships. Many sections speak about this.[1] It was also noted that there are many references to the phrase 'one another'.

A study of the 'one anothers' of the New Testament shows us that there are clearly two groups of words. To put it succinctly there are the supportive 'one anothers' and the corrective 'one anothers'. The first is a set of 'one anothers' where I enjoy the relationship with the other person. Here the other person is in a giving mode and the attitude towards me is one that I appreciate. The second is a set of 'one anothers' that I have difficulty accepting or receiving. Here the other person is calling for a response from me in ways that will most likely demand a change in my behaviour (see Figure 1). The first group bring encouragement and inspiration to my life, the second development and accountability. The first encourages me to 'keep it up' and the second to 'sort it out'. The first is the 'carrot', while the second is the 'stick'. Parents will appreciate that it is necessary to use both 'carrot' and 'stick' in the nurture of children. So it is in the nurturing of our Christian life. Sadly, we often find it difficult to give and receive both forms of assistance. Unfortunately some people are too insecure in their relationships to give, while other people are too insecure in their relationships to receive.

It is significant that there are more supportive 'one anoth-

Supportive 'One anothers' You give to me I feel comfortable Brings encouragement & inspiration 'Keep it up' The 'carrot'	**Corrective 'One anothers'** I need to respond I may feel uncomfortable Means development & accountability 'Sort it out' The 'stick'
accept (Rom 15:7) be at peace with (Mk 9:50) be compassionate to (Eph 4:32) be devoted to (Rom 12:10) be kind to (Eph 4:32) be like-minded towards (Rom 15:5) be patient (Eph 4:2) bear with (Col 3:13) belong to (Rom 12:5) build up (1 Thess 5:11) carry burdens of (Gal 6:2) consider others better than yourselves (Phil 2:3) Do not bite and devour (Gal 5:15) do not go to law (1 Cor 6:6) do not grumble about (Jas 5:9) do not judge (Rom 14:13) do not lie to (Col 3:9) do not provoke & envy (Gal 5:26) do not slander (Jas 4:11) encourage (1 Thess 4:18) forgive (Eph 4:32) greet (Rom 16:16) have concern for (1 Cor 12:25) have fellowship with (1 Jn 1:7) honour (Rom 12:10) live in harmony with (Rom 12:16) love (John 13:34) offer hospitality to (1 Pt 4:9) pray for (James 5:16) serve (Gal 5:13) show humility towards (1 Pt 5:5) speaking to (Eph 5:19) wait for (1 Cor 11:33) wash feet of (John 13:14)	admonish (warn) (Col 3:16) confess sins to (Jas 5:16) spur on (provoke) to love (Heb 10:24) submit to (Eph 5:21) teach (Col 3:16)

Figure 1. Supportive and corrective 'one anothers'

ers' than there are corrective 'one anothers' by a ratio of about 7 : 1. Carrots need to be more frequently administered, but sticks must not be ignored.

> **Many of us would rather be ruined by too many compliments, than rescued by a little criticism.**

I recall two instances, of many, in my own life when 'stick' and 'carrot' events were experienced.

The first was an evening when the leadership team of our rapidly growing congregation was meeting together. We were on a weekend retreat at a beach house high above the ocean. The waves were pounding on the beach below us with a dull roar. It was a cloudless night and the moon was nearly full. There is something magical about moonlight on surf.

The eight of us had gathered to review our progress and plan for the future. We had also set time aside to 'speak into' each other's lives. It was my turn to be 'spoken into'. I was being accused of being too domineering within the leadership group. I did not think it was true. It was very painful. My pride was hurt. I was confused, hurt, angry, defensive. My feelings were far from the tranquillity of the idyllic surroundings of that moment.

Sleep was difficult that night, not because of the roar of the pounding surf but because of the turmoil within.

I arose early next morning, slipped out of the beach house and went for a walk down the road high above the beach. The sun was just rising, the tide was out exposing huge areas of sand. The noise of the waves was ceaseless – a constant low drone. My mind was still wrestling with the accusations of the previous evening. Maybe I should resign. A break from full-time pastoral ministry would be good. I could very happily go back to my Science teaching. I poured out my heart to the Lord, tears flowed.

As I walked down the road lost in thought, my attention was drawn to a property being developed some thirty metres back from the road. It was literally being cut out of the rocky hill. A flat region, just large enough for a beach home had been exposed and foundations were being established. The drive up to the property was steep and rough. It was evident that the work was long and hard. It was probably being carried out by the owner in his spare time and at weekends.

> *Iron sharpens iron (Prov 27:17).*
> *Side by side sharpens – head to head blunts.*
> *So it is in human relationships.*

The gentle voice of the Holy Spirit spoke to me, not audibly but deep within. 'Brian, anything that is worthwhile takes time, effort and pain. Why do you react to your brothers' comments? If they are wrong, you stand clear in your conscience before me. If they are right, they are pointing out blind spots that you cannot see. Spots you would wish me to deal with if I were here.'

A deep sense of peace engulfed me. I looked away from the building site to the beach scene below and worshipped. One more rough edge of character had been rubbed off. A further insight of kingdom truth had been understood. A new area of freedom had been embraced. I would be tested again in this area but the ice had been broken – next time it would be easier.

The further experience was in a house group in our own home. The people present had been divided into smaller groups and each person was asked to share two or three positive things about the other members in the small group. In my group was my oldest son and two women from our congregation. It was a moving time as we spoke of the things that we appreciated in each other and then prayed together.

The emotions felt on these two occasions were very different. The first was an intense struggle for me – feelings of hurt and anger were close to the surface. I felt like running away, whereas the second was supportive, heart-warming and stimulating. The first was calling me to accountability, while the second was bringing me encouragement. Today as I look back on my life I am glad that I have had people around me who have been prepared and able to relate to me on both the corrective and supportive relationship levels.

*We judge ourselves by what we feel capable of doing,
but we judge others by what they have already done.*

We see these two aspects of relationship in the life of Jesus in
his relationship with his Father. Was he accountable in his
relationship to the Father? Yes! He always sought to do the
Father's will. Scripture tells us that he learned obedience by
the things that he suffered (Heb 5:8). Was he encouraged by
the Father? Yes! At his baptism the heavens opened and the
Father said, 'This is my Son, in whom I am well pleased.'

My observation is that most Christians are weak in both of
these areas of relationship. The easiest should be in compli-
menting and encouraging each other but we often neglect
this. There seem to be several reasons for this neglect.

> We are too busy.
> We are unobservant.
> We are self-absorbed.
> Our standards are too high of others. They are normal-
> ly lower for ourselves.
> We are too self-conscious.
> We are frightened others may become proud – we are
> there to keep them humble!

Some of the most moving times that I have experienced have
been amongst young people at weddings or birthdays. I well
remember one wedding. After the formal speech-making
during the wedding breakfast the floor was opened to anyone to comment about the young couple. One after another
young people rose to compliment and praise their peers.
There was deep sincerity, genuine love and real appreciation. Some times there were tears of gratitude and hugs all
round. It was a time of great inspiration, encouragement and
blessing to everyone – listeners, receivers and givers alike.

*We need to cultivate accountability – 'How are you
getting on?' and vulnerability –
'How am I getting on?'*

In the more difficult area of accountability many in the
Christian church have been put off because of the abuses

they have experienced themselves or witnessed in the lives of others. Heavy-handed authority, especially shown by insecure leadership, can be very harmful. This is not what I am advocating. On the other hand, all 'carrot' and no 'stick' in relationships within a congregation will not produce mature character. Our job is not to see through others, but to see others through. To bear our brother's and sister's burden, not to bare it to others around. The 'sorting out' aspect of congregational relationships was taken so seriously by Paul that he indicated relationships should be severed for a time until repentance occurs (1 Cor 5:11–13).

Encouragement can be given by anybody to anybody at any time. One does not have to know the person well to bring words of encouragement. However corrective relationships can only function when there is trust between people and trust takes time to develop. We need to voluntarily place ourselves in positions of accountability so that our Christian faith will mature. We need to develop relationships with people whom we can trust, who have our best interests at heart and who are not afraid to 'speak the truth in love' (Eph 4:15) to us. We need to cultivate attitudes such as transparency, honesty and humility. It is not easy, but it is essential. We need to cultivate accountability – 'How are you getting on?' and vulnerability – 'How am I getting on?' Such relationships are even more important among leaders – we will look in more detail at this in a later chapter.

> *Our chief need in life is someone who can make us
> do what we can.*

Here are some simple guidelines for corrective relationships.

- Invite this form of relationship from a few respected and trusted friends. Encourage these people to focus on the five corrective words listed in Figure 1.
- Schedule special times when this can occur.
- Listen carefully – you do not have to agree but you must promise to think about, evaluate and pray about what is shared with you. The worst thing that can happen in this situation is that we fly to our own   defence   and

seek to justify our actions.
- If in doubt about what is being suggested, seek further confirmation, if possible from other sources.
- When you recognise that what these people are saying is right, tell them that you agree, thank them for their courage and get them to pray for you.
- Ask them to monitor your progress in the areas that they have commented on.

There is great security and blessing within such relationships. I believe God intends that we love each other, trust each other and are honest with each other so that we can help each other grow. Whether or not we are able to develop and handle such relationships is a measure of our maturity as Christians.

Some years ago I was put in charge of a Science Department. I am a firm believer that the teaching of science should be one of the most interesting school curriculum subjects that children can ever be exposed to – no apologies to teachers of other disciplines! It was therefore my intention to establish a stimulating environment in which to train teachers. One of the areas of science that is of interest to both men and women is the polishing of rocks so I decided to purchase a 'tumbler'. A tumbler is basically a small drum with a rubber lining that is attached horizontally to an electric motor. Rocks are placed in the tumbler, then water and an abrasive grit are added. The tumbler is firmly closed, the motor started and the whole unit is left running. The grit, water and rocks rotate hour after hour. After about two weeks of continuous running the motor is stopped and the tumbler is opened. Inside you find a soupy solution that is poured away, leaving rocks that have lost most of their rough edges revealing something of their colour. Fresh water is now added and further abrasive grit, this time of finer texture, and the process repeated. Round and round the tumbler goes, rumbling and vibrating – everybody knew when the science students were tumbling their rocks! The next time that the tumbler is opened the rocks are starting to become quite interesting. Their colours glisten, their rough edges have all gone and they are becoming very attractive. The process is repeated one more time with still finer abrasive grit. The final opening of the tumbler is always an event of great excitement – what will the rocks finally look like is on everyone's mind. There they are absolutely beautiful! Sparkling, gleaming, colourful gems, ready to be made into jewellery.

As I was pondering this process one day I came to see that this is what a congregation is. It's a tumbler full of rough-hewn stones – Christians – of untapped potential. Add some abrasive grit – the circumstances of life. Add water – the ministry of the Holy Spirit and tumble – for days, weeks, even years. That is how God crafts Christians. It is a painful process being tumbled together. It would be so easy to decide to sit isolated on the bench in the laboratory in an attempt to become a gem but it does not work that way!

It is only in God's tumbler that gems are formed.

4

LET'S PARTY

When I was a student I sometimes used to take a twenty-five-minute bus trip to university. I have always been a keen observer of human beings and during the trip I can well remember observing those around me in the bus. The business person – reading the newspaper. A teenager – earphones on, eyes closed, tapping their fingers to the music. I could hear it as well! The senior citizen – dozing. A fellow student, diligently reading her textbook, catching up on last minute study. The young mother – tightly clutching her children. People gazing absent-mindedly ahead, looking out the window, avoiding eye contact with each other. A bus is a place where people have no desire whatsoever to establish relationships with those around. They are transient, fellow-travellers who have been thrown together by a quirk of chance or fate – here as a matter of convenience, with little concern for those around. Such a place must be second only to a lift as a place of impersonality, a place that islands of humanity are from time to time forced to endure. Now consider a party. Imagine the people there; laughing, moving around, fraternising, interacting, talking, listening, relaxing, sharing their lives with each other. A party is a place where people choose to go to enjoy themselves, to be with people they know. Hard to imagine two environments more totally different isn't it? Buses and parties. Should a congregation be more like a bus or a party? Well, I have declared my hand with the title of this chapter, even if in our congregational services we sit facing the same way as we do in a bus!

A party is an event that provides social and emotional enrichment. It is where relationships are the main reason for the occasion. People want to celebrate an event or a milestone with friends – you cannot party by yourself. Whereas a bus has another primary purpose – it is simply a convenient way to get from one place to another. It is not set up to enhance relationships.

Unfortunately some congregations are like buses – people go to them to get from one place to another, from earth to heaven. There is little relationship – it serves a different purpose. As we have already shown, the New Testament indicates that the central purpose for the congregation is to bring people together. For them to share their common life and celebrate key events that contribute to their pilgrimage as members of God's kingdom.

> *'Human beings, like plants, grow in the soil of acceptance, not in the atmosphere of rejection.'*
> *John Powell*

There are five key supportive 'one anothers' that contribute to our 'party'. They demand our closer consideration and seem to be absolutely crucial for healthy congregational relationships. These are:

> honour one another
> forgive one another
> encourage one another
> accept one another
> love one another

As we consider these five aspects of relationships, think of a beautiful flower garden and the intertwining of the various factors to create that beauty; the sun – beaming down, bringing light, revealing the beauty of the plants ('honouring one another'); the rain – gently falling, refreshing, washing off dust and particles ('forgiving one another'); the fertilisers –

bringing nutrients, creating luxuriant growth ('encouraging one another'); the bees flitting from flower to flower – of little concern to them is the colour of the flower, whether it's a daffodil or a rhododendron, how tall the 'plant may be or whether it comes from South America or South Africa ('accepting one another'); the soil – the basis of it all, the foundation and place from which all of the life of the garden originates ('loving one another').

Honour one another

'Honour one another above yourselves' (Rom 12:10).

Norman Vincent Peale some years ago told the following story. (I hasten to add that it could equally as easily have been told about two men!)

> In a little mill town, years ago, as a young minister assigned to my first church, I found the congregation split down the middle by one of those feuds that sometimes start with two stubborn contestants and wind up with everyone taking sides. The leader of one faction was an irresistible force named Mrs Follett. The head of the other was an immovable object named Mrs Lloyd. Things had reached the point where the two groups sat on opposite sides of the aisle and glared across at each other.
>
> Drawing on my vast inexperience, I was all for calling on both the women and pointing out their Christian duty to stop hating each other. However, a member of the congregation, a rugged old mill worker named Rowbottom, stopped me.
>
> 'It will not work,' he insisted. 'You'll just make things worse. A conductor of good will, that's what the minister of a church should be. Goodwill is much stronger.'
>
> 'But how does one transmit goodwill,' I objected, 'if there is not any in the first place?'

Rowbottom tapped me earnestly on the shoulder. 'Create some, boy,' he said. 'Create some!' And he walked away.

I knew that hostility provokes hostility, that anger breeds more anger, and that the church was caught up in this vicious circle. As I pondered Rowbottom's words, it occurred to me that the converse might also be true. If either of these two embattled women could be persuaded to say something remotely pleasant about the other, perhaps the downward spiral could be reversed.

The difference between stumbling blocks and stepping stones is how you use them.

In those days full of zeal, I made a great many parish calls. And since I weighed only sixty kilos wringing wet, the good women of the parish were forever offering me glasses of milk and pieces of pie or cake 'to keep me from blowing away' so they would say. One day, sitting in Mrs Lloyd's living-room, I took my courage in both hands and remarked that on the previous afternoon I had enjoyed a piece of pie at Mrs Follett's house. I added casually, 'She's a good cook, isn't she?'

'Hmph!' simmered Mrs Lloyd. 'She's a good cook all right. If her disposition were only half as good, we could all be thankful!'

Half an hour later I was in her adversary's kitchen with a plate of homemade biscuits balanced on my knee. 'Mrs Follett,' I said, after a few preliminaries. 'This morning I heard Mrs Lloyd say something nice about you.'

'Who?' cried Mrs Follett incredulously.

'Mrs Lloyd. She said you were a good . . .' (here I crunched a happy mouthful) '. . . cook. As indeed you are.'

'Well!' said Mrs Follett. 'Well, I never! I suppose if it comes to that . . .' (she tossed her head as if she could-n't believe what she heard her voice saying) '. . . Peggy

Lloyd has a light hand with pastry herself'

You can imagine where my parish calls took me the next day and what message I passed on. And feeble though this little flicker of goodwill was, it was the beginning of the end of that church feud. Rowbottom was right; love is stronger than hate, affection is more powerful than enmity, hostility is not a natural state of affairs. Most people want to escape it and feel better when they do.

Although all those involved benefited from my little experiment, the chief beneficiary was myself. It introduced me to my favourite hobby: being a relay station for the little sparks of goodwill that otherwise might never jump the gap that separates people.

> *'When someone does something good, applaud!*
> *You will make two people happy.'*
> **Samuel Goldwyn**

Ricochets! That's the mechanism I use. Most of the time it's just that of the second-hand compliment. I have trained myself to listen for any word of approval or praise that one individual speaks about another – and pass it on.

It's so easy! It can be done in casual conversation the next time you meet the person who was complimented. It can be worked into a telephone call. It can be part of a letter, or all of a hurried note.

And it's so rewarding! The originator of the friendly thought benefits from the gratitude of the person who receives it. The recipient's need – and we all have this need – is met in a happy and unexpected way. And you, the person-in-the-middle, have the satisfaction of knowing that because of your effort, a little flash of goodwill has been released into the environment.

This story is an example of the importance of honouring one another. Honouring each other is something we don't do very well. Often our society tends to honour people for all the wrong reasons. We honour fame, money, position, power, film stars and sports stars. Many people who have grown up without any honour or respect in their families, feel no sense of value and self-esteem. The media contributes to this lack of respect for other people, it so often heaps scorn on important areas such as marriage, authority and moral values.

Honour has to do with recognising the value of people. We can honour others in two ways. Firstly by verbal expressions when we praise, applaud, acclaim, compliment and acknowledge them. Secondly by our attitudes whereby we respect, appreciate, admire, esteem, value, cherish and have a high opinion of others. Of course attitudes of the heart should precede any words we may express. We honour people when we encourage them to do things for us and for others. In congregational life this means allowing people to use their natural talents, acquired skills and spiritual gifts for each other. To honour others is to make them feel valued and the focus of attention, not ourselves. We are urged to humbly 'consider others better than yourselves' (Phil 2:3) and to 'honour one another above yourselves' (Rom 12:10). This is something we do not very easily relate to. Often as individuals we are self-centred rather than other-centred. Our society has made us competitive and we do not normally honour those we are competing against. E. Stanley Jones says that

> The most miserable people in the world are the people who are self-centred, who don't do anything for anybody except themselves. They are centres of misery with no exceptions. On the contrary, the happiest people are the people who deliberately take on themselves the sorrows and troubles of others. Their hearts sing with a strange wild joy, automatically and with no exceptions. We are structured for the outgoingness of the love of the Kingdom. It is our native land.[1]

Again we have the example of this aspect of relationships in the Trinity where we see that the Father, Son and Spirit honour each other. In that passionate prayer of Jesus (Jn 17) we hear him saying the following:

- You glorify me and I will glorify you (v 1)
- 'I have brought you glory on earth by completing the work you gave me to do' (v 4)
- 'And now, Father, glorify me in your presence with the glory I had with you before the world began' (v 5)
- 'All I have is yours, and all you have is mine. And glory has come to me through them' (v 10)
- 'I have given them the glory that you gave me' (v 22)
- 'I want those you have given me to be with me where I am, and to see my glory, the glory you have given me because you loved me' (v 24)

Among other things, to glorify means to honour. The Father honours the Son, the Son honours the Father. Jesus said that the Spirit 'will testify about me' (Jn 15:26), 'he will bring glory to me by taking from what is mine and making it known to you' (Jn 16:14). To testify means to bear witness, to recognise or to acknowledge. The Spirit recognises and acknowledges the worth of the Son and points us to his worth. The Father and Son send the Spirit (Jn 15:26). They acknowledge, respect and honour what he does. There is never any competition, feeling of inferiority or insecurity between the members of the Trinity. They each know and respect who they are and who the other members are and they honour each other.

> *People may not be as good as you tell them they are but they will try harder thereafter.*

What a great 'party' we would have if we honoured each other more. What a difference honouring each other more would make in unstable marriages or families, in our committees and the governing bodies of our congregations, between local churches and denominations, between different national or cultural groups. Dare I say it, between the English and the Irish, the Americans and the Canadians or the Australians and New Zealanders? How different our attitudes would be to the congregation down the road if we allowed the ministry of the Spirit to challenge us and change us in this way towards them. For us to respect them, praise them and have a high opinion of them. This is the passion of Jesus for our relationships.

I recall someone in our congregation coming to me after a service and saying how much they appreciated the worship team that morning.

'Do not tell me,' I said, 'go and tell them, they need to hear that from you.'

'Oh do you really think I should?' was their reply!

It is strange that we find it hard to genuinely honour others. It seems that it is something we all need to learn to do.

There is a spectrum of attitudes that we can have towards other people

To esteem   To tolerate   To despise

When it comes to those in our congregation, small group or leadership team, the New Testament is very clear about this matter, we must move to the left of this spectrum.

Let's honour one another – let's party!

Forgive one another

'Forgiv[e] one another, just as in Christ God forgave you' (Eph 4:32).

There is one thing most certain in life – sometime, somewhere and probably quite often, people are going to hurt us either intentionally or unintentionally. They will do things to us or say things to or about us (or others) that we do not agree with or approve of. These actions can become like cancers – rampantly dividing cells – that threaten to squeeze the life out of relationships between people.

> *'Forgiveness is the fragrance the violet sheds*
> *on the heel that has crushed it.'*
> *Mark Twain*

Over the years I have decided that I am not responsible for what others do to me or say about me. I am responsible for how I react to what they say or do. Their action is their responsibility, my reaction is my responsibility. It is all too possible for my reaction to another person's action to be just as bad.

Something else that I am still learning in life is that often people do not realise the full implications of what they are doing to us or saying against us. Both Jesus – 'Father forgive them for they know not what they do' (Lk 23:34 RSV) and Stephen – 'Lord, do not hold this sin against them' (Acts 7:60), permitted this realisation to change their attitude towards the perpetrators of their deaths.

> *'Forgiveness is not an elective in the curriculum*
> *of life. It is a required course,*
> *and the exams are always tough to pass.'*
> **Charles Swindoll**

Thus, part of forgiveness means that I release the other person from my personal judgment of his or her motives and actions. It does not mean that I condone the action – I would not have done that, they should not have done it either. It means that I will not allow that action to become a double sin, once on the person's part for doing it to me and the second time on my part in my reaction to it.

How many people in congregations harbour unforgiveness? I am afraid its presence is all too frequent. Unforgiveness breeds bitterness, anger and resentment. These are enormously destructive emotions in relationships and often produce physical symptoms as well.

Judy[2] was often in constant pain through arthritis. She had been to numerous doctors and specialists and had tried many different remedies. During counselling one day she was encouraged to face a deep attitude of unforgiveness that she had towards family members. Painfully and courageously she confronted it, acknowledged it and released it through prayer and ministry. Over the next few weeks she was wonderfully healed from her arthritis. Such is the power of forgiveness, touching mind, spirit and body.

> *Because nothing we arrange is flawless, and nothing we attempt is perfect, and nothing we accomplish is faultless – forgiveness is an essential ingredient of living.*

We are to forgive because God has forgiven us. Our sin was an affront to the holiness of God. It was God's grace that enabled him to bring us forgiveness, it will be our humility that will enable us to forgive others.

If I have made a mistake, criticised, acted vindictively or thoughtlessly towards another person, then I need to apologise and seek their forgiveness and the other party needs to show forgiveness.

Forgiveness is like a cleanser in relationships; it deals with the grime and rubbish that accumulates.

Let's forgive each other – let's party!

Encourage one another

'*Therefore encourage one another and build each other up*' (1 Thess 5:11).

In some ways honouring one another and encouraging one another are similar responses. I include both as they are essential components in healthy relationships.

> *Honour is given for what has already been done, encouragement for what is currently being done.*

When we honour others it may be more of a public activity, whereas encouragement is more often at a private one-to-one level. Honour comes after accomplishment in the past, encouragement is necessary to keep going in the present and the future. Honour is for what has been done, encouragement is for what is being done. Honour is for who we are, encouragement is for what we are becoming. Of course honouring another also brings encouragement to them. As with honour so with encouragement, they are often sadly lacking in our congregations.

As a leader in our congregation, from time to time I receive little notes or cards in the mail. Sometimes they are anonymous, sometimes the writers sign their name. They come with encouragement, thoughts, verses, words of support and inspiration. What a blessing! And so often just at a most appropriate time. The word 'encourage' means to put 'courage into', and we all know that this is true.

What great value there is in encouragement. What a marvellous contribution it can make to our 'party'. It is particularly important when things are difficult. 1 Thessalonians 5:11 was written by Paul after he had had to hurriedly withdraw from the city of Thessalonica leaving young Christians there who were facing difficult times. In the midst of this he said 'Encourage one another and build each other up'. Encouragement does that, it builds us up, fortifies us to hang on, helps us realise that what we are doing is worthwhile.

How easy it is to do the opposite; to grumble, murmur, complain. Human beings seem to have a bias towards criticism, complaining, grumbling, negativism and blaming others. Our news media thrives on this human trait – bad news is good news so far as the press is concerned; it sells many papers and helps improve television ratings. In my earliest days of teaching I remember an older staff member once saying to me, 'Brian, 5 per cent problem will always overshadow 95 per cent possibility.' I have lived to discover just how true this statement is.

Moses discovered just how destructive and pernicious grumbling could be as he led the people of Israel towards the Promised Land. Listen to the people within three days of crossing the Red Sea.

'Moses, why do we have to drink this water? It's foul' (Ex 15:24).

They had just seen an amazing miracle, the sea had parted, they had walked through on dry land and their enemies had been destroyed and yet they were complaining! Even so God did another miracle and sweetened the water.

Listen to them grumbling again six weeks later.

'Moses we are starving. Why did you bring us out here to

this wilderness to die? It would have been much better to have stayed in Egypt, at least we would have died with full stomachs' (Ex 16:2). So God gives them manna and quail.

A short while later they are grumbling again.

'Moses it's your responsibility to get us some water. Our children are thirsty, our animals are dying.'

'How can I provide enough water for all of you?' answers Moses, 'Go and find your own water' (Ex 17:3). So God commands Moses to strike the rock and water flows.

Now they stand on the borders of their promised land. The spies had returned with a majority report that they faced impossible odds. What did they do? Listen to them.

'For goodness sake Moses, you bring us all this way only to find that there are giants in this so called promised land. Now we will die. Our wives will be ravaged and our children become slaves. It would have been better to die in the desert. We are going to elect another leader and go back to Egypt' (Num 14:2).

Grumble, grumble, grumble. Think about it! They had seen enemies defeated, water sweetened, quails and manna provided, water gushing out from a rock, the awesome events of Mount Sinai – all miraculous events from the hand of God and yet still they grumbled. However, we dare not criticise the Israelites, we also find it very easy to complain about things.

> *'I complained because I had no shoes,*
> *until I met a person who had no feet.'*
> **Arab Proverb**

Such attitudes within a congregation cause it to spiral inwards. They are terribly destructive, divisive and debilitating. It is very difficult to reverse the downward path of disillusionment in someone's life, such a path is accelerated by others around about complaining and grumbling. That is why God says, 'Encourage one another!' It is like fertiliser to a plant.

That the New Testament places a high priority on encouragement is seen by the use of the Greek word *parakaleo*. This word, or its derivative is used in the following ways:

- It is one of the names given to the Holy Spirit – 'encourager' (Jn 14:16, 26; 15:26; 16:7).
- Encouragement is a special gift given to the Church (Rom 12:8).
- The word is used twenty-five times in the book of Acts. More times than the word for baptism is used.
- Barnabas was the Son of Encouragement (Acts 4:36).
- The gift of prophecy is given for encouragement (1 Cor 14:3).
- Tychicus was specially sent to Colosse and Ephesus to encourage the Christians in these places (Col 4:8, Eph 6:22).
- Timothy was sent to Thessalonica to encourage the Christians there (1 Thess 3:2).
- God encourages us so that we can encourage others (2 Cor 1:4).
- Paul was constantly giving encouragement. He says his 'purpose was to encourage' others (Col 2:1–2).
- Paul draws much of his own encouragement from others (2 Cor 7:4, 1 Thess 3:7).
- Paul commands Timothy and Titus to encourage others (2 Tim 4:2, Tit 2:15).
- Elders were to be encouragers of others (Tit 1:9).

Encouragement is verbal sunshine.

Encouragement reinforces our community life (1 Thess 4:18, 5:14, Heb 10:25). It builds up people in their faith (1 Thess 3:2, 5:11). It strengthens us to live out our Christian faith (2 Thess 2:16–17). It brings refreshment and unity (Rom 15:5, Phm 7).

Here are some simple suggestions that I would encourage (it's that word again!) you to seek God's grace to put into action:

- Look for the things that God is doing and rejoice in them; in your life, in your family's life, in those within your congregation. God is always doing something.
- If things are difficult, choose to be part of the answer,

not part of the problem. Ask, 'What can I do to help and encourage others in this situation?'

- If you believe in a God who answers prayer, then pray. Why grumble when you can pray?

- Listen attentively to people. When someone really takes an interest in me and listens attentively to what I have to say, it is a very affirming and encouraging experience. It gives me the feeling of worth and belonging. A story is told of a man trapped inside a pocket of air in the hull of an upturned fishing boat. After tapping for hours trying to communicate with those outside he was overcome with relief when he finally heard his rescuers tapping back. 'At last people knew where I was,' he said after being rescued. That's what good listening does, it means people know where I am.

- Engage in the three levels of verbal encouragement –

    Thanks – for what someone has done.

    Praise – for how they have done it.

    Honour – for who they are.

Interestingly we are to respond to the greatness and goodness of God on the same three levels.

Encouragement – if you cannot see the bright side about anything polish the dull side.

- Remember, that just as there are seasons in nature so there are seasons in relationships, in family life, in congregational life. I have yet to discover a single congregation that has everything together in one place at the one time. I have a sneaking suspicion that God plans it that way to keep congregational leaders humble and prayerful! Be patient, become an encourager.

What happens in a family when things get tough? When a son or daughter has a broken relationship, their sports team loses, a child breaks an arm or they are turned down at a job interview. What do we do? We encourage them! This is an important aspect of life.

Encouragement also plays an important part in the development of Christian character. There will always be plenty to discourage us with ourselves, with our congregation and with those around us. We need to encourage those in leadership – congregational leadership is a very difficult task nowadays and it appears to be getting more difficult. We live in an age when leaders in society are the focus of much criticism. Pastors and ministers are resigning and returning to business or industry. Others feel worn out by the high demands and pressures of the job. They need heaps of encouragement.

We need to encourage those working with youth and those teaching children. We need to encourage parents, teenagers and young marrieds. Those in single parent families need special encouragement as do singles. We need to encourage those whose ministry is one of prayer, giving and teaching God's Word. We need to encourage those in front-line ministries in our own country and overseas.

Do you bring other people up or down?

No one can ever get too much encouragement. Let us commit ourselves to the noble task of encouragement.

Let's encourage each other – let's party!

Accept one another

'Accept one another, then, just as Christ accepted you' (Rom 15:7).

When I was a student in high school we had an unfortunate individual in one of our classes whose nose was constantly running. A blob of thick moist mucus always seemed to be hanging from the end of his nose. As you can imagine, others in the class would try to avoid sitting beside him and he was the centre of considerable ridicule. Teachers would often request him to blow his nose. He gained an unfortunate nickname – we called him 'honey'! I apologise if this illustration offends you, but it graphically illustrates the next point I wish to make.

Have you ever considered why it is that we call other people names? You know – nerds, weirdos, pommies, male chauvinists, feminists, anti-abortionists, wogs, fundamentalists or whatever. Human beings are very good at dreaming up labels for various groups of people. It is simply a reflection of the fact that they are different to us and we do not accept them.

We human beings have a great difficulty accepting those who are not like us. We feel threatened by variety; we are much happier being with people who think as we do, act as we do and speak as we do. When one travels from country to country, cultural differences become very obvious and sometimes embarrassing. We have a tendency to look down on the way other people do things and at the same time feel that the way we do things is the only way of doing it. Unfortunately, this problem is seen in our congregational relationships as well. We are quick to label people as conservative, reactionary, liberal, charismatic, dispensationalist or whatever.

One of the greatest threats to society today is the emphasis on what separates us rather than what brings us together.

I well remember (many years ago I am pleased to say) the consternation expressed by some 'mature Christians' when one hot summer Sunday morning a young Christian walked into our Communion service with no shoes on! It did not help that he had also very long hair! He was not our type of person, he did not do things the way we did them. Of course the way we do things is the way that God does them! How hard it is for people to adjust and to accept others' attitudes, actions, lifestyle or theology.

Acceptance is the second 'one another' we are urged to embrace which has its example in Christ. We are to accept each other because Christ has accepted us. We are totally safe with God. He accepts us not because we behave like him but because we are of value to him. Romans 5:8 says that 'God demonstrates his own love for us in this: While we were still sinners, Christ died for us.' God did not love us according to our behaviour. Even though we had offended God's holiness, he still accepted us. No matter what a person does, they have value to God. Yes, that includes Hitler and Idi Amin. Every human being has equal value in the eyes of God because each of us is created in his image. Unfortunately the image has been fatally flawed by sin and this is often evidenced by various forms of errant behaviour. Because we all have equal value to God, he therefore accepts each human being equally. Nothing you or I can do, say or think will ever shock God. On the other hand we are often shocked by the things that people do, believe or say. Such shock or disapproval normally becomes evident by our reactions. People do not feel accepted and so are not safe with us. We need to see people through God's eyes – of equal value – and accept them on this basis not on the basis of 'acceptable' behaviour.

I remember another event within our congregation when members of the fellowship discovered that there were non-practising homosexuals in our congregation. It was so hard for them to accept the fact that such people should worship with us.

For healthy relationships we need liberal doses of acceptance. Sometimes we want to play God. To have to show people that they are wrong and sort out their lifestyles. However, that is God's job, it is the work of the Holy Spirit to convict people of sin. We may become God's agents in this ministry, but only if we are invited to do so. We are all learning, we are all imperfect, always. We all make mistakes, we are all maturing in God. One of the things we must learn to do if we are going to have successful relationships is to learn to live within the framework of other people's weaknesses, then what they do will not surprise us.

God is a God of variety. He delights to put us in teams and congregations with the most unlikely people. Often we cannot choose the people we work or worship with in a congregation or leadership team. The church has been likened to a body; many different parts with different functions (1 Cor 12). It is also like an orchestra with many different kinds of instruments, all making a valuable contribution to the harmonies produced.

In New Zealand we have two types of forest. Many square kilometres of manmade Pinus Radiata forests where all the trees are identical, but very boring. Then there are the Native forests with huge variety, texture and colour – magnificent examples of the creativity of our Maker. It is of little surprise that people normally choose the latter to walk through. Nature shows diversity. Diversity is also God's plan for the Church.

Nice illust-ration

> **'Unity can only be seen in diversity not in conformity.'**
> **Jurgen Moltmann**

God's desire is that people of both sexes, of different economic status and different cultural background, all relate together in congregational life (Gal 3:28). Despite this clear indication of God's commitment to diversity in nature and within Scripture, we still argue for the formation of homogeneous congregations that convey to people that they are unacceptable. We form youth congregations or cultural congregations; people drawn together because they have 'like interests' and feel more comfortable in such groupings. They prefer meeting with 'their kind of people'. My personal belief is that such groups should only function for the purpose of outreach and evangelism. People are best evangelised by those from similar background and culture with whom they relate more easily. They find it easier to become Christians without crossing racial, linguistic or class barriers. However once people have entered the kingdom of God, every effort should be made to enfold them into broader-based congregational groups in appropriate ways.

I would be the first to acknowledge that this is not easy and seems to be becoming increasingly more difficult by the year. However the principles of the kingdom of God and wrestling with our acceptance of one another, must never be sacrificed for the pragmatic reasons of church growth. Obviously the greatest limiting factor is that of language. Where people cannot speak to each other there is very little chance of meaningful relationships. Thus language-based congregations may be necessary, at least until adequate cross-communication can be established.

Maybe Stevie Wonder also had congregations in mind when he wrote, 'Ebony and Ivory, together in perfect harmony'!

Let's accept each other – let's party!

Love one another

'A new command I give you: Love one another' (Jn 13:34).

There is no doubt that this command, repeated sixteen times in the New Testament, embraces all the others. Love is the cardinal Christian quality. Love is central to the character of God – God is love, God loved so much that he gave his Son. Love is the fruit of the Holy Spirit. Love is at the heart of the first two commandments – 'Love the Lord your God . . . and your neighbour as yourself.' Three times in the New Testament we read that the whole of the law is summed up in these two commandments (Matt 22:39–40; Rom 13:9; Gal 5:14). Keep these and you keep the whole law. Three things endure – faith, hope and love. But the greatest of these is love.

So much has been said and written about love that there is little else to do except to do it!

Love equals care. It can be described as 'wanting the highest good of another'. The world's type of love is 'because of' love. I will love you because you agree with me. I will love you because you are good enough. I will love you because there is something in it for me. This is insincere love. We are told that 'love must be sincere' (Rom 12:9). The New Testament type of love is 'in spite of' love. I will love you in spite of what you are or what you have done. It is a 'laying down of our lives' type of love. The love of the Good Shepherd for his sheep (Jn 10:11).

We are to 'provoke each other to love' (Heb 10:24). The word 'provoke' literally means paroxysm, that is to excite, stimulate, arouse, inspire, stir, incite, galvanise. Love is one of the qualities we are to both show to one another and also inspire in one another. It is both a supportive 'one another' and a corrective 'one another'.

> *'Love that is not expressed in loving action does not*
> *really exist, just as talent that does not express itself*
> *in creative works does not exist; neither of these*
> *is a state of mind or feeling, but an activity,*
> *or it is a myth.'*
> **Sydney Harris**

Some years ago I was involved in a small group Bible study being lead by a well-known English conference speaker. As we were discussing the verse, Hebrews 10:24, we were all moved to hear this man of God tell about an experience he had one evening while taking a bath. He was one of those bathers who love to splash around and slop water everywhere, much to his wife's annoyance – she had to clean it up after him. As he was sitting there one day rubbing his back and slopping water around to his heart's content this phrase hit him like a ton of bricks – 'Provoke one another to love'. He realised in an instant that his current behaviour was anything but 'provoking his wife to love' so from that day on he has cleaned up his own 'sloppy' bath water!

If there is any group of people on this earth who should be able to demonstrate what love is, it should be Christians. God has given us other Christians as a test of our love. Our life is found in God, the source and author of love. Our Master showed what love really meant. Our guide book is full of it. Our congregations should be living examples of this important quality. Unfortunately this is so often not the case. Watch what happens at the first sign of controversy or disagreement. Sometimes we give the impression that our loving of others depends on whether or not they have the same theology as us. If you cross all your theological 't's and dot all your theological 'i's, then I'll love you.

Jesus prayed that the Father's love be in us, 'that the love you have for me may be in them' (Jn 17:26). His longing is that his love be ours, 'Love one another. As I have loved you,so you must love one another' (Jn 13:34). Love is also the ministry and fruit of the Holy Spirit. Think about it – the love the Father had for the Son is to be in us, the love of Christ in us, the love of the Spirit in us! This is God's intention – the Trinity at work in the life of individual believers creating love. Oh that this would be our goal and prayer. What a transformation it would bring in congregations around this planet. Little wonder that Jesus said, 'By this all men will know that you are my disciples, if you love one another' (Jn 13:35). I wonder why we do not set this as our highest priority in congregational life. We have so many other goals; growth, buildings, finances, evangelism, mission. I wonder how many congregations around this planet have ever set their goal for the year to love each other as Christ loved them. This is the new commandment. The commandment that embraces all others. It is the desire of God. Francis Schaeffer once said, 'Love among Christians is the final apologetic. It is the definitive mark of the disciples of Jesus,' and yet we don't make it ours – sad and strange.

Love doesn't make the world go round, but it does make the ride worthwhile.

It is recorded that a common statement made by the first-century society as they observed Christians was, 'Look how these Christians love each other'. What would it mean if the twentieth-century society were to observe the same thing in modern congregations.

Robert Lupton was called by God to work among the poor in Atlanta, USA. In a book called *For Theirs is the Kingdom*, he recounts insights that the poor taught him. Reflecting on some of the issues we have been discussing he has this to say about John 17.

When the meeting was over, the Teacher closed in prayer. 'Father, make them one. Make them so much a part of each other that when one hurts, they all feel the pain. Make them inseparable, as loyal to each other as you and I are loyal to one another. May their commitment to each other be so real, and visible that there is no doubt their love is not of an earthly kind. Make them the very reflection of the kind of unity and glory we have together in heaven. Then the world will know for sure that I was sent from you. Amen.'

(John 17:11–21)

Then he was gone. Taken from them in a whirlwind of events: an arrest, the cross, the resurrection, the ascension. But what he left behind was so strange and wonderful it was beyond human imagination. In the trust of a couple of commercial fishermen, an inland revenue agent, a former prostitute, a doctor, a businesswoman, a political activist and an assortment of mostly low-income, uneducated folk he left the keys that would open the entire world to his kingdom. He entrusted to them his New Commandment and a new power, the Holy Spirit, who would enable them to obey it. He would use them and their simple obedience as a means to reveal himself to the world. It would not be their wise words but their unusual commitment to each other that convinced the world of his deity.

The Teacher has been gone for quite some time now. In his absence some confusion has arisen. Certain of his followers have taken the position that the Great Commission is more important than the New Commandment. They have developed remarkable strategies to evangelise entire cities and nations. They have devised ways to broadcast his words from powerful satellites in the heavens. They have learned to grow successful churches by grouping together all the people who are alike. In fact, because they have become wealthy and powerful, they can do almost anything they desire to promote the kingdom.

The problem is that the active love demanded by the Teacher cannot be adequately communicated through television studios. Deep commitment to one another is

not observed in proliferating the printed word.
Homogeneous churches do not reflect a unity that dif-
fers from other groupings common to this world. In
skipping over the tough demands of the Teacher, we
have forfeited the very power which he said would
prove his deity to the world.

Admittedly, it is easier to mouth loving words into a
microphone than to confront someone who has offended you. It is more stimulating to do creative programme
planning than to wrestle through one's own self-centredness and prejudice. Worship and fellowship in the
comfort of the familiar is so much more pleasant than
the hard work of laying down one's own liturgical or
theological preferences for the sake of a brother or sister. And the homogeneous approach to kingdom building is marketable. It is selling well.

Power has its limits, it cannot control love.

I suspect, however, that when all is said and done the
convincing, life-changing power of the kingdom will be
experienced right where the Teacher said it would be –
where the lives of his diverse followers are laid down
for each other. Perhaps the world will catch glimpses of
his reality when:

– his efficient ones are inconvenienced by the slow;
– the bright ones lavish their valuable time and talents
    on the ignorant;
– those who have much sacrifice for those who do not
    have enough;
– those who normally separate from each other on the
    basis of IQ, skin tone, age, or earnings lace their
    lives together intentionally, inseparably, for the
    sake of their Teacher.[3]

So that's the church as a party – a place of relationship and
celebration.

Would more people be interested in our Jesus if we his followers were better at 'partying?' I wonder.

Let's party.

5

I'll do it my Way

My friend Ken,[1] was telling me about a phone conversation
he had just had with the husband of a newly married couple.
There had previously been some tensions between him and
the wife of the man but he believed that these had been
ironed out. The phone conversation went something like
this.

'Hi this is Ken, how are you?'

'OK. What do you want?'

'I have rung to say that I met a friend of your wife's recently and she wanted me to pass on her regards to Kathy.'

'We don't need you to pass on anybody's regards. As far as
we are concerned we don't want to hear from you.'

'Oh . . . er . . . er . . . what's the matter?' stuttered my friend,
totally taken aback by this announcement.

'You know what the **** matter is! Kathy never wants to
see you again. We don't **** trust you.'

'But I thought Kathy and I had sorted things out!'

'You know that things are not **** sorted out. You never
sort **** things out, you just take, take, take all the time. How
your wife can ever live with we don't know! You're just a
domineering pig, the **** lowest form of life that we know!'

And so it went, on and on. A torrent of abuse and curses.
Hatred, bitterness, unforgiveness and hurt all jumbled into
one. What a vicious grip it had on their lives. It had left Ken
very shaken, he was still quite agitated when he arrived at
my home.

> **So live that you are not ashamed to sell your parrot**
> **to the village gossip.**

Not a very noteworthy event you may think. Just a micro-cosm of what happens in our society when relationships break down. It never ceases to amaze me how quickly rela-tionships can deteriorate and to what depths they can plum-met, often bringing out the worst emotions, motivations and language imaginable.

Against the possibilities painted in the previous chapter, we come back to what are so often the stark realities in many human relationships. We need to address the depth of the problem that faces us. What is the problem that hinders us from achieving what the intentions of God are for his people and the passion of Jesus?

What's the problem?

Maybe you feel that you do not have any problems with rela-tionships. Then I suggest you try to remember how you responded the last time to the following situations:

- How did you react when you were right and someone told you that you were wrong?
- How did you react when you were wrong and someone told you that you were wrong?
- How did you react when someone else was wrong and you had to tell them?
- How did you feel inside when someone else got the credit for something you had done?
- How did you react when your reputation was threat-ened?
- How did you react when after doing you best, helping others and serving God nobody noticed?
- Did you find it easy to apologise to
  - strangers?
  - friends?
  - spouse/parents?

• How did you react towards those in your congregation who disagreed with what you believed?

> *The heart of the human problem is*
> *the problem of the human heart.*

No doubt all of us would recognise reactions surfacing within ourselves in the above situations. What do these reactions tell us about ourselves? How would Jesus have responded to these situations? One does not have to be a Christian very long before we realise that there is something within us that opposes the purposes and plans that God has for us. Our human nature is flawed and human relationships, even Christian ones, are all too often tense and strained and sometimes irreparably damaged.

Independence the root

Where does this problem come from? What are its roots? Why are we afflicted in this way? What is it that rises up in us and so often gets in the way of our best intentions?

The source of this problem is summed up in one word – 'independence'. At its heart, this is what sin is – independence from God. The essence of the fall was men and women's arrogant desire for autonomy. Both the fall of Satan and the fall of Adam and Eve were as a result of wanting to be like God. That is, to be independent from God. Or, putting it another way, out of relationship with God. Created for interdependence, people choose independence. Created to be God-centred, we have become self-centred. This self-centredness is easy to prove. If you look at a photograph that you are a member of, who do you look at first?

Theodore Roosevelt, president of America, never underestimated his own importance. Reflecting on their father, one of the children is reputed to have said. 'Father always had to be the centre of attention. When he went to a wedding, he wanted to be the bride. When he went to a funeral, he was sorry that he couldn't be the corpse.'

The worst failure in life is the lack of self-discipline.
Self-discipline has to be learned from adults,
it does not come instinctively.
Children must learn it from adults.
To tell an adolescent that it is OK to follow their
impulses is to point that child down
the road signposted 'disaster'.

We have four children, and it did not take us long to realise that that little idol of our parental eye, that bundle of love, smiles and innocence had its own way of announcing its independence. We do not have to teach children to start running the other way when Mum calls, or to stamp their little feet in defiance, or scream in rebellion in the shopping centre. Children are not called the 'terrible twos' for no reason! It is not something that children have to learn, they just seem to do it – strange that! There is an inner problem here; it comes very naturally.

We are all born with a self-centred nature and for many of us this independence is reinforced by our rugged, cultural individualism, best described by the phrases 'doing my own thing', 'getting my own way', or 'standing up for my own rights'. Further, we live in an age when Satan has deluded people into thinking that the first sin – independence – has turned into a virtue.

We see evidences of this independence so clearly within people in the following actions and attitudes – competition, jealousy, pride, ego, selfishness, dissension, arrogance and covetousness. All of these express problems in human relationships. Nowadays it is popular to talk about self-worth, self-expression, self-interest, self-esteem – we have become obsessed with ourselves. One of the main roles of a parent is to change a child from a self-centred individual to an other-centred individual. Self-centredness is at the core of our pluralist society.

We see this self-centredness and self-obsession taken to an extreme in advocates of New Age ideas where we hear people saying that they find God in themselves or, worse, that they are God. We were created to love God but instead of that love being focused outwards towards the Creator, it has become a boomerang bending back to focus on ourselves. People's loving being focuses attention back on self. What was meant to be directed to God is now directed towards self.

Talk to someone about themselves and they will listen for hours.

Self-centredness the fruit

Scripture says that a particular plague of the last days will be the love of self –

> But mark this: There will be terrible times in the last days. People will be **lovers of themselves**, lovers of money, boastful, proud, abusive, disobedient to their parents, ungrateful, unholy, without love, unforgiving, slanderous, without self-control, brutal, not lovers of the good, treacherous, rash, conceited, lovers of pleasure rather than lovers of God.
>
> (2 Tim 3:1–4 my emphasis)

There is the core of the problem; lovers of self, rather than lovers of God.

In these verses this love of self is seen as a problem, it gets in the way of loving God. It is popular today to encourage people to 'love themselves'. We are told that unless people 'love themselves' they cannot love other people. This idea is based on the words of Scripture where we read, 'Love your neighbour as yourself' (Lk 10:27, Rom 13:9, Gal 5:14, Jas 2:8). James says that is the royal law (Jas 2:8). However I am not so certain that Scripture endorses the love of self, rather it just recognises this fact. It is saying that we should care for others with the same degree of intensity as we care for ourselves. Paul uses the same phrase in Ephesians 5:28 when he says, 'He who loves his wife, loves himself.' He then goes on to say that, 'No-one ever hated his own body, but feeds and cares for it.' He is not necessarily endorsing the 'love of self', he is using it as an illustration.

> *As human rights have been demanded, human*
> *responsibilities have been demeaned.*

Lest I am misunderstood on this, let me hasten to say that I am in agreement with the **intentions** of those who say we need to love ourselves before we can love others. It is very clear that the way we view ourselves will affect the way we relate to others. We need to have a healthy view of who we are, before we can have healthy relationships with others. The biblical view seems to be that as Christians our identity is in Christ. He is both our creator and our redeemer. Our focus is outward, it is towards Christ, not inward towards ourselves. Maybe we are using the incorrect terminology when we encourage people to 'love themselves', particularly in the light of this warning in 2 Timothy 3:2, where loving self can become a barrier to loving God.

Notice the list of human behaviours between these phrases talking about last-days people 'lovers of themselves' and 'rather than lovers of God' – boastful, proud, abusive, disobedient, ungrateful – all of them relationship problems. It's fashionable to say that we are living in the last days – maybe we are. All I know is that I have not lived during any other age and the relationship problems mentioned in the above verses seem to be happening nowadays, and in abundance.

This self-centredness is a fruit from which springs the competitive nature that we will examine in the next chapter. James writing to early Christians, highlights the problem of competition and self-centredness when he says, 'For where you have envy and selfish ambition, there you find disorder and every evil practice' (Jas 3:16). He says these attitudes are not from heaven but from the devil. Little surprise then that they create disorder!

> *For the last twenty years the church has*
> *emphasised self-fulfilment in Christ rather than*
> *self-denial with Christ. For seeds to multiply*
> *they must first die.*

Maybe the story of Narcissus should be a warning to us in this matter. Having resisted the charms of all others, he one day came to a pool of clear still water. Bending down to drink he was struck by his own reflection. He admired the face, the hair and eyes and fell in love with himself. Unable to embrace, kiss or talk to his love, he pined away and died.

My rights the priority

As has so often been noted, today's society is preoccupied with 'rights' rather than 'responsibilities'. We have human rights, gay rights, animal rights, women's rights, children's rights, rights of the unemployed, land rights and abortion as a woman's right, to mention just a few. People are all out to get what they think is theirs and seldom think much about what they can contribute to society or to others. Such an outlook and philosophy contains the seeds for the destruction of democracy. The great principles of our democratic society were not built on seeking rights but recognising that we could do things better if we co-operated together. Democracy is not about rights, it's about responsibilities. Or, as President Kennedy put it, 'Ask not what your country can do for you but what you can do for your country.'

Individualism has become a virtue in our society and the 'rugged individual' is the idol. There is nothing wrong with being an individual. God has created each of us as unique individuals. God respects and loves the individual. Each of us is created as an individual in the Maker's image. Each human individual has dignity. The problem comes when we add 'ism' to the word 'individual'. We then end up with an ideology. Individual becomes individualism, capital becomes capitalism, feminine becomes feminism, human becomes humanism, material becomes materialism, nation become nationalism and race becomes racism. Nothing wrong with being human, having capital or being feminine, it's the ideology that is the problem.

God loves individuals but hates individualism. Our society is becoming unhinged. We are intensely self-centred and competitive. If we all embrace the ideology of individualism then the weak will become the prey of the strong and we will return to the rule of the jungle.

Denominationalism is the surrender to the ideology of our culture – individuality.

Currently this planet faces an intense outbreak of nationalism. Nations want autonomy and cultural groups crave recognition of their identity. To a degree this is a healthy expression of God-given uniqueness but it also contains the seeds of destruction and conflict. It engenders most of the conflicts that we witness on earth – Serbs against Croats, black against white, Israel versus PLO, the elimination of six million Jews during World War II. We have witnessed the disintegration of the USSR and its replacement with the Commonwealth of Independent States. Will this fragile union survive, or will it splinter further into feuding blocks? Given human nature, the future is not optimistic.

The Bible talks about the heart – not the organ that pumps our blood round the body but the seat of the real person, the inner self. It is seen as the centre of our affections, motives, thoughts and attitudes. It is also called the old self, the old nature or the flesh. We read that the 'heart is deceitful above all things and desperately wicked' (Jer 17:9 NKJV). We are told to 'put off your old self, which is being corrupted by its deceitful desires' (Eph 4:22). We have an incredible capacity to deceive ourselves.

I once talked to a Christian man whose marriage had tragically broken up. Well prior to his divorce he had taken up sexual relations by living with another woman, also a Christian, saying they 'could not wait'. He maintained they still loved the Lord and that God had shown them that what they were doing was right in his eyes. When we deal with deceit, here is the greatest danger. 'Deceit', by definition means we do not know that something is happening to us. We are deceived into self-centredness and individualism!

Why is it that so many of us in the Christian body cannot get on together? Why is it that we so often want to do our own thing and often find it difficult to work together? These problems are rooted in our sinful nature, our uncrucified egos and desires for self-glory. It is not only the rapists or murderers in our prisons that have deceitful hearts, Christians have them as well.

> ***When people are wrapped up in themselves they make pretty small parcels.***

Maybe next time we are in a tense relationship situation with a fellow member of the body of Christ it would be well to ask the following questions.

- Why am I feeling this way?
- Why am I doing these things?
- Is this separating people or uniting people?
- Whose glory am I seeking?
- Is what I am saying (doing) being divisive in this situation?
- Am I putting the wedge in or am I taking the wedge out?
- Is this breaking down or building up?

Answers to such questions will often show us the nature of the problem residing in us.

Being in pastoral work and watching people's reactions over many years one learns a lot about human nature. It always saddens me when people who are struggling in some relationship situation are not prepared to discuss it. They do not want to see you or talk to you. When you try to approach them to talk about the problem they get their nose out of joint and then sometimes leave the congregation. This is a reflection of our independence and self-centredness.

Then there are the very spiritual versions of individualism. The 'I only listen to God' people. Or the 'I do not need to go to church to be a Christian' people. If God meant us to mature in him by going it alone why did he give such a variety of gifts in other people to help us grow?

I have discovered that diagnosis is the first step to remedy. Knowing that I struggle with self-centredness and understanding that this affects my relationships, enables me to better deal with the problem.

It is to solutions that we will turn in a later chapter. Next we will see how competition becomes so destructive in relationships.

BEING NUMBER ONE

They were walking towards Capernaum, the Master and his disciples. As was often the case the Master was some distance behind, engaged in talking to those who approached him on the way. The disciples were further down the road arguing among themselves.

'Why do you, Peter, James and John, get special treatment from the Master? What makes you better than us?' demanded Judas. 'Just yesterday he took you three with him up the Mount while we were landed with trying to heal that man's demonised son. Anyway my responsibility of looking after our finances is much greater than any of your responsibilities. I deserve greater recognition.'

An egotist is an 'I' specialist and conceit is
a form of 'I' strain.

'Looking after the money is no big deal,' snapped Peter. 'You can't even do that properly, you didn't budget adequately for the recent taxes. If the Master had not come through with the fish with that coin in its mouth where would we have been? Anyway, I was one of the first disciples chosen by the Master and he used my fishing boat to preach to that crowd by Lake Gennesaret. That gave me the right to go up the Mount with him yesterday.'

'You wouldn't have even been with the Master if I had not introduced you to him,' replied Andrew.

'Special privileges because he used your dirty, smelly fishing boat?' snorted Matthew, 'I gave the Master the greatest banquet he has ever had. Now that was real class. What has a smelly fishing boat got on that? It was . . .'

Simon the Zealot butted in, 'Well I don't know about fishing boats and banquets. I believe the Master is looking for men with some fire in their bellies – people who have got what it takes when it comes to dealing with those who try to get in the way. If you want my opinion there are too many wimps in this group.'

'Being wimps is not the problem,' shot back Thomas. 'The problem with this group is that too many have their heads in the clouds. When all is said and done what the Master needs is practical down-to-earth people like me.'

As they reached Capernaum the Master caught up with them and together they entered the house of a friend.

'What were you arguing about on the road?' he asked them. There was a stunned silence among his disciples. He knew they had been arguing! How could he? He had been so far behind them busy talking to people. Eyes diverted, consciences quickened, hearts beat faster.

> *'Whenever I get full of myself, I remember a nice,*
> *elderly couple who approached me with a camera one*
> *day. When I struck a pose with them, the man said,*
> *"No, no we want you to take a picture of US." '*
> **Actor, Tom Selleck**

'Why do you argue among yourselves about who is the most important?' asked Jesus.

Not only did he know that they had been arguing, he also knew what they been arguing about. Embarrassing! Gently Jesus took a small child in his arms and said, 'Anyone who wants to be great in the kingdom of God must become like this little child.'

Arguing about who is the greatest in the first century (Mk 9:33–37, Lk 9:46–48) has to be the same as 'competition' in the twentieth. If first-century disciples were caught in the powerful web of one-upmanship, then so are twentieth-century disciples.

Competition – not a characteristic of God's kingdom

How incredibly competitive our society has become. Competition has become so much part of it that we barely give it a second thought.

Children are taught to compete at a very young age. They run races in school, someone wins and someone has to come last. Teenagers experience competition – peer pressure is just a sophisticated term for it. Buying a pair of jeans for the teenager? Then any old pair will not do. They must have the right label! It must be the height of audacity that clothing companies can charge the parents of teenagers to buy their products and then get free advertising whenever they are worn!

> *'The proud count their newspaper clippings –*
> *the humble their blessings.'*
> **Bishop Fulton J. Sheen**

Competition will drive athletes to permanently harm their bodies by taking performance-enhancing drugs. Competition will sometimes cause science researchers to adjust their results in order to produce conclusions that will enable them to receive grant money. Once in every four years the eyes and ears of whole nations are held captive as they urge their competitors on in the Olympic Games. Political parties are subject to competitive pressures, both from within the party and from without. Multinational companies will re-locate whole industries off shore because of competition.

Competition affects us all; we compare ourselves with others according to how big our bank balance is, how fast we can run the hundred metres (or the marathon!), how tall we are, our IQ, our grades in music exams, the type of profession we are engaged in, the car we drive, which suburb we live in, our looks, our position in the company, our singing ability, the house we own, the clothes we wear, where our team finished in the tournament, the qualifications we have, the countries we have visited, our weight. Just about anything

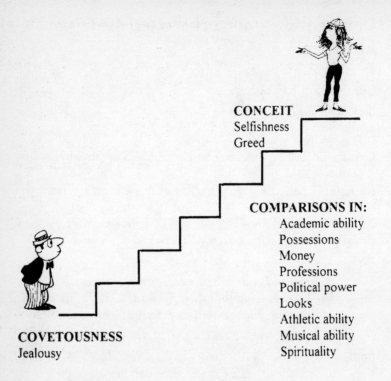

CONCEIT
Selfishness
Greed

COMPARISONS IN:
Academic ability
Possessions
Money
Professions
Political power
Looks
Athletic ability
Musical ability
Spirituality

COVETOUSNESS
Jealousy

Figure 2: How competitiveness affects us.

we own or whatever abilities we have are capable of being graded according to society's criteria of success and failure.

Then there is the *Guinness Book of Records* that one can attain fame in by attaining to obscure achievements. Such a document bears silent testimony to the preoccupation humanity has with competition. Being the first, going the furthest, making the biggest, becoming the fastest, these are the things that drive many people in our society.

It is as if we place ourselves on staircases or ladders of attainment (see Figure 2) and compare ourselves with those around us. So-and-so is better looking than me, but I have more brains. I have a degree, they only have a diploma. They drive a BMW, I only have a Honda. And so it goes on.

It's dangerous to be concerned with what others think about you.

We are constantly in danger of comparing ourselves with others around us across a wide range of abilities and assets. We try to decide whether we are better or worse than they are and where we fit when it comes to attainments. Advertising thrives in this environment. We so often become jealous or covetous towards those who have more than us or are more able in certain areas. Or we may become conceited if we have more than others or are more able or successful than they are. We do not normally say this, at least not in so many words – that is not socially correct – and often we may be quite unaware that we are doing it and what is happening to us.

Competition, and its half-brother comparison, are very destructive attitudes. Many of society's ills lie at their doors. How many suicides have occurred because the people have looked at themselves and felt that they failed to meet society's criteria of success? How many marriages break down because of competition between spouses? How much sibling rivalry is due to competitive attitudes?

A competitive spirit, linked to jealousy, was the main reason for Cain killing his brother Abel. How much unpleasantness is generated in the workplace because people are competitive? There must be something wrong with a system where my winning depends on another losing. This cannot be the kingdom of God. Fortunately there is some recognition coming of the insidiousness of highly competitive societies. Nowadays we have people talking about 'win-win' situations. Here neither parties in the relationship are disadvantaged by a decision.

There is a children's story called *Hope for the Flowers*[1] that reminds me of the problems that competition brings. It is about an ambitious caterpillar named Stripe who decided to climb to the top of a mountain of caterpillars. These caterpillars were all climbing over one another, trying to get to the top. As Stripe plunged into the pile and began his ascent, he asked, 'What's at the top?'

Another climber responded, 'No one knows, but it must be awfully good because everybody's rushing there . . .'

Stripe soon found that moving up the mountain was a struggle. He was pushed and kicked and stepped on from every direction. It was climb or be climbed. But Stripe disciplined himself neither to feel nor be distracted as he continued to push his way up.

'Don't blame me if you don't succeed! It's a tough life. Just make up your mind,' he yelled to any complainers.

Finally, Stripe neared the top of this huge mountain of caterpillars. As he looked ahead, he saw something disturbing; a tremendous pressure and shaking was sending many at the top crashing to their death below.

Stripe felt awful with this new knowledge. The mystery of the pillar was clearing – he now knew what always must happen on the pillar. Frustration surged through Stripe.

As he agreed that this was the only way 'up' he heard a tiny whisper from the top: 'There is nothing here at all!' It was answered by another: 'Quiet, fool! They'll hear you down the pillar. We're where they want to be. That's what's here.'

Stripe felt frozen. To be so high and not be high at all. It only looked good from the bottom.

> *When you put yourself on a high pedestal, and feel that you are above the rest of the world, just remember that the size of your funeral will depend a lot on the weather.*

That is what competition does to us. It absorbs our time and energy and when we get to the top we find what we have attained is of little ultimate value.

Unfortunately competitiveness also creeps into the Christian Church and is all too prevalent among individual Christians – spiritualised competitiveness of course! We may compare our gifts with those of others, our spirituality, our Bible knowledge or our preaching ability and often grade ourselves accordingly. In charismatic and Pentecostal circles, spiritual authority and power are valued commodities. All too often we grade people's effectiveness by these criteria. We compare our congregation with other congregations around us. In an age when church growth is important, ministers and pastors have become very protective and competitive when it comes to those attending their congregation – numbers of people attending a congregation are important. They are a modern-day measure of success, a scale of attainment. People move from congregation to congregation looking for something better, seeking something more exciting. It is a big temptation for church leaders to seek to cater for these urges and try to create a church environment that outdoes the congregation down the road. You can grade churches' competitiveness by reading the advertisements in the church notices of the newspaper about their Sunday services. I once read an advertisement that started – **'Come to Auckland's most exciting church'**. If that's not competitive I

v21 *"The eye cannot say to the hand, 'I do not need you!'"*

v15 *"... foot should not say, 'because I am not a hand I do not belong to the body.'"*

Fig 3 A New Testament view of competitiveness (1 Cor 12)

do not know what is!

Comparing ourselves with others must be the most point-less and destructive exercise that any Christian can ever engage in. It plays right into the enemy's hands in tempting us to conceit on the one hand and covetousness on the other.

Competition is a terribly destructive force in Christian rela-tionships. How many church splits have been created because people have compared their congregation with another? How many church leadership teams have been split because of competitive attitudes between leaders? How many people are wandering from congregation to congrega-tion comparing one with another and trying to find a better church?

Paul refers to this problem in 1 Corinthians 12 where he explains how the body (of Christ) functions. He says that there are many parts which make up a whole. No part is per-mitted to compete or compare itself with any other part. There is to be no **superiority** in the body of Christ – 'The eye cannot say to the hand, "I don't need you!" ' (1 Cor 12:21). Neither is there to be any **inferiority** – the foot must not say, 'Because I am not a hand, I do not belong to the body' (see Figure 3). The clear teaching of the New Testament is that each Christian is totally unique and does not need to com-pete with any other Christian.

The four big 'C's' that affect us all are – competition, which leads to comparison which leads to either conceit or cov-etousness (Figure 3).

Christians cannot live their lives in isolation.
We need a community of friends who will challenge
our drift towards self-deception.

The Church of Jesus Christ should be the safest place on earth – safe from competition, safe from comparisons. Paul refused to compare himself with others and criticised those who did, saying that they were not wise (2 Cor 10:12). There should be no need for conceit or covetousness. Each person should be able to be just who they are in God. The congrega-tion should be a place of mutual support and encouragement. Growth in gifts, abilities and Christlikeness should be the goal of each person for themselves and in turn they should be contributing to this in each other.

Such is the picture Paul paints in Ephesians 4:12–16. Gifts are given to the Church – 'to prepare God's people for works of service . . . body of Christ may be built up . . . reach unity . . . become mature . . . attaining fullness of Christ . . . no longer be infants . . . grow up . . . [be] held together . . . builds itself up in love, as each part does its work'. Each part has a part. There is absolutely no place for competition, comparison, covetousness or conceit here. This is God's idea of a 'win-win' situation. He designed such a system long before twentieth-century personnel managers came along.

Uniqueness is God's fingerprint in creation. God is into 'one offs' not 'carbon copies'. As far as we know each snowflake is different. If God put such uniqueness into snowflakes how much more does he put this quality into human beings.

There are over eight million different ways that the twenty-three pairs of chromosomes in a female cell can be selected to form the egg (mathematicians will know that this is 2^{23}). Similarly there are over eight million different ways the twenty-three pairs of chromosomes in the male cell can be selected to form the sperm. Any one of these eight million arrangements of sperm can fuse with any one of the eight million arrangements of egg. This means that there are sixty-four million, million ways of arranging the twenty-three pairs of chromosomes in the new individual – more than all of the people who have ever lived on planet earth! Talk about each human individual being unique – God has not yet exhausted all the possible combinations for creating human beings. This magnitude of uniqueness is possible without even considering mutation, chromosomal crossovers or environmental factors that will add even more possibilities for diversity.

The biggest cemetery is where all the unused
talents lie buried.

Different – not better or worse

In 1 Corinthians 12:4–6 we are told that there are different kinds of gifts, different kinds of serving and different kinds of empowering. Different – not better, not worse. Each congregation of God's people should be a celebration of 'differentness' – unique gifts and abilities functioning in unity and harmony – now only God can do that!

An appreciation of these facts should diffuse many of the relationship problems that so often spoil the life of a congregation. If we could just grasp the fact that we are a team. That there is no place for competition or comparisons in the body of Christ – here the operative word is another 'C' word – '**cooperation**'. The glorious truth is that by releasing the giftings of others around me, I enhance my own gifting. This is the way God has made us to function. It is vital that every member of a congregation, a leadership team or a small group knows this. It takes a huge pressure off us. Incidentally, teaching children the difference between 'being the best' and 'doing their best' will take a huge pressure off them in our competition-driven society.

Recognising the differences between us does not mean that we need to cover up weaknesses and inadequacies. We all have weaknesses just as we all have strengths. The key to strong Christian relationships is to cover for each other's weaknesses and release each other into our strengths. This is not the way our competitive society functions. In society another's weaknesses are exposed and exploited. Normally the knife is ruthlessly put in. In society we criticise strengths and seek to pull people down into mediocrity. Not so in the kingdom of God! An understanding of the principles of the kingdom of God makes such responses totally inappropriate among Christians.

Humility a key

To function in the ways that I have been suggesting within the Christian family means we need to come to a humble and honest assessment of ourselves. Humility is a prime Christian virtue, a virtue often misunderstood and frequently explained away in Christian circles.

I am not to be infatuated by my strengths,
neither am I to be intimidated by my weaknesses.

Humility is not some condescending doormat-like position that a Christian is supposed to take. A truly humble person feels neither superior nor inferior to others. A truly humble person is free from comparison and competition. Jesus humbled himself to come to this planet (Phil 2:8) – he knew exactly who he was. He did not have to pretend he was someone else. He did not need to compare himself to others or compete with them. Neither did he place himself on a scale of 1 to 10 against others. We are told to have this same attitude. It was never God's intention for us to place ourselves on some gradient of achievement. Sin and self-centredness have created that competitive problem.

At its core, and by definition, competition is self-interest. You do not normally compete to help someone else achieve better results than yourself. Economists may wax loud and long about the benefits of a competitive, free-market system. There is no doubt that this is probably the best way to run an economy within a fallen system, but at its core is competition, and competition has the individual's interest as its raison d'être.

The meaning of the Greek word for humility is to '**be on the plane**' – the opposite of being on some scale, staircase or ladder of achievement. Being on the plane means we do not see ourselves above what we really are nor do we see ourselves below what we really are. We do not have a superiority complex, neither do we have an inferiority complex. We are not proud, boastful, arrogant autocrats, neither are we cringing, whimpering, snivelling little worms.

The doctrine of grace humbles people without
degrading them and exalts them
without inflating them.

In Romans 12:3 we are instructed to think of ourselves with 'sober judgment' – another translation says 'have a sane assessment of yourselves'. I like that. I am able to recognise my strengths and my weaknesses. I am not to be infatuated by my strengths, neither am I to be intimidated by my weaknesses. That is true freedom. The Romans 12 portion is associated with gifts given to the body of Christ. We are encouraged 'not to think of ourselves more highly than we ought' (v 3). We are told that we have all been given 'grace' by God and this grace is expressed in his gifts given to each of us (v 3). God has made me. He has given me strengths and abilities. There are things that I can do well. There are things that others do well. I do not need to feel threatened by others' abilities. Thinking more highly than I should about myself is an unrealistic assessment of myself. I think I am better than others. Thinking too lowly about myself is an unrealistic assessment of myself. I think I am not as good as others, and these two things, stifle God's best for me. We are reminded 'that each member [of the body] belongs to all the others' (v 5). Notice, no competition, no comparisons – just humble co-operation. That is God's intention for his people, may we grasp it with both hands.

> *Everything that God has done for us may be summarised in one word – 'grace',*
> *everything that we do in response to him may be put in another word – 'gratitude'.*

We often hear Christian people saying they are proud about what they or their children, their congregation or their mission has achieved. I would like to suggest that pride is not a suitable response for a Christian. Gratitude is the only suitable response for a Christian.

- Gratitude for one's upbringing, for the strength and the abilities given.
- Gratitude for the grace and gifting received from God.
- Gratitude for the opportunities to achieve.
- Gratitude acknowledges that the source of ability is

> outside of one's self – that it is sourced in God, the
> giver of all good gifts.
> • Gratitude cuts at the root of pride.
> • Gratitude centres in God, the focus of our Christian
>   life.
> • Gratitude acknowledges that achievements are God-
>   centred and not self-centred
> • Gratitude undermines the competitive urges.
> • We are told to give thanks in all things (1 Thess 5:18).

As Christians we are urged to do everything for the glory of
God not the glory of self, family, church or mission. God's
special grace is upon the humble (1 Pet 5:5–6) but he resists –
stands against – the proud. Think about it – being proud
means God stands against us!

Andrew Murray beautifully expresses what true humility
means –

> Humility is perfect quietness of heart. It is to expect
> nothing, to wonder at nothing that is done to me, to feel
> nothing done against me. It is to be at rest when nobody
> praises me, and when I am blamed or despised. It is to
> have a blessed home in the Lord where I can go in and
> shut the door, and kneel to my Father in secret, and am
> at peace as in a deep sea of calmness, where all around
> and above is trouble.

Surely this was the quality of humility that characterised the
life of Jesus.

Many relationship problems could be quickly resolved if
humility were present. Just think how often we find it hard
to apologise and how this has contributed to prolonged
strain in relationships. Pride is probably the most powerful
reason for not apologising. Pride is one of the reasons that
people refuse to resolve issues, preferring to hold onto their
own hurts, to maintain walls and to continue to hurt others.
We all do this to each other in some way or another. We will
be returning to study the topic of humility at greater depth in

chapter 8.

The Holy Spirit reveals sinfulness not to condemn but to cleanse and establish humility.

It is particularly significant that in responding to the disciples' competitiveness that day on the road to Capernaum, Jesus took a little child to illustrate the meaning of true greatness in the kingdom of God (Matt 18:1-4). A little child (probably aged three or less) – unpretentious, having no sense of self-importance, where the competitive urge has not yet been sharpened up. Jesus said 'Whoever humbles himself like this child is the greatest in the kingdom of heaven.'

Dealing with our competitiveness and pride has a triple blessing. It enhances our relationships with one another, brings God's grace and blessing and also brings true greatness in the kingdom of God.

What greater motivation could we have?

7

SHOT IN THE FOOT

Nazareth was abuzz with excitement. The Teacher and his followers had been seen in a nearby town and it was obvious they were heading their way. The people of Nazareth had heard of the miracles – perhaps he would do the same here. Maybe he would heal someone or change some more water into wine, that would give them a great excuse for a party.

So it was, the Teacher arrived in town.

There was a large crowd at the synagogue that Sabbath. It had been said that the Teacher always went to the synagogue on the Sabbath and the people of Nazareth were full of expectation and keen to hear what he had to say.

They were not disappointed. His teaching was unlike anything they had heard before. Clear, with authority, good illustrations and most of all bringing insight and life. Amazing – the time just flew by.

'How did he get all this knowledge?' they whispered among themselves.

'He is the carpenter's son, isn't he?'

'Didn't his father live here in Nazareth?'

'Isn't Mary his mother, and aren't his brothers and sisters here?'

'He just lived around the corner from the synagogue, didn't he?'

'I remember him making that chair for me. So how come he knows so much?'

'He didn't have any special training, did he? How has he

been able to do miracles?'

The questions flew around the crowd as Jesus continued to teach. Uncertainty began to creep in.

'I do not agree with that point,' said one neighbour.

'No, neither do I,' replied the other.

'What right has he got to say those things?' asked the third.

The people of Nazareth were starting to see the Teacher in a different light. Doubts were surfacing, resentment and pride were raising their heads. The leaders of the synagogue were not slow in fanning suspicions and supporting the rising tide of resentment as they drifted around among the people. Their consciences were being pricked by the Teacher's instruction on that Sabbath. They were jealous of his popularity. The synagogue leaders never got such big crowds when they taught on the Sabbath.

If human beings accepted each other many of the world's problems would disappear.

The Teacher recognised what was happening that day among the crowd. Actually he had half expected it. The last time he had been here in his home town the people had tried to throw him over a cliff when he had finished reading from the book of Isaiah. He had wondered what sort of reception he would get when he returned. He had hoped that perhaps as a result of his widely acclaimed ministry since his previous visit people would have been more likely to accept him. However, it was not to be. He paused and with a deep sigh said,

'Only in his own home town, among his relatives and in his own house is a prophet without honour.' With that he concluded his teaching and sat down.

There would be no miracles that day among the people of Nazareth. There was no faith and this amazed the Teacher.

A day or two later he moved on to the next village. The town of Nazareth could relax. The leaders of the synagogue could return to their own uninspired teaching and the people of the town to the things that preoccupied them. The Teacher had passed them by, never to return. They would hear further reports about the miracles he did in the villages around, but now they ignored them. It was only Jesus the home-town boy.

What was it that caused the people of Nazareth to react that way to Jesus? How could they acknowledge and marvel at the wisdom and miracles but still dismiss him?

This event illustrates several of the points covered in previous chapters. The reaction that those in Nazareth had to Jesus is unfortunately very common among people. Several words highlight the response; familiarity, prejudice, jealousy and pride.

> *'Those who hate don't win unless you hate them –*
> *and then you destroy yourself.'*
> **Richard Nixon**

Notice the following points about this event in the life of Jesus, see how each builds towards the next. This event was about halfway through the ministry of Jesus. Many people had heard his teaching and seen his miracles. His reputation had been going on before him, he had become quite well-known. As far as those around Galilee were concerned he could no longer be dismissed as an inexperienced novice.

- The people in Nazareth recognised his gifting. They were amazed to hear about Jesus' teaching and miracles. There was a genuineness about Jesus. There was no question about his authenticity and credibility. What he was doing had been validated, he was no con man.
- Prejudice became a barrier. They could accept what Jesus was doing but not who he was. He was from their own town, he was one of them, they all knew his family. This was Nazareth, how could any good thing come out of Nazareth? Good things had to come out of Jerusalem, never out of Nazareth. There was that feeling of inferiority within the townsfolk, 'Nazareth has nothing to offer and if it did, it couldn't be from that man. We are all common people in this town. How can he have gifts and abilities that we don't have; he couldn't

have learnt this in Nazareth.' So the tall-poppy destroyers got to work. They had pre-judged Jesus. Pre-judgment – that's what prejudice is.

> ***Unbelief is the darkroom of our soul where we develop our negatives.***

- Prejudice generated unbelief. The people's unbelief seemed to genuinely take Jesus by surprise. Unbelief is such an uncompromising attitude; it is cynical, critical, arrogant, self-confident, narrow-minded, immovable and pessimistic. It has no gentleness or sympathy and it most certainly lacks optimism and expectancy.
- Unbelief limited God's blessing in Nazareth. Amazing really, the power of the Son of God limited by the unbelief of those around him. The Messiah himself, directed by the Father and empowered by the Holy Spirit, could not do many miracles among these people. What a tragedy for that town!
- Jesus left and went to other towns (Mk 6:6). The Son of God left Nazareth and moved on. There was almost a sense of resignation, or sadness about this statement. His own people could not accept him, he turned and went to others who would.

The above event in the life of Christ is recorded in both Matthew (13:53–58) and Mark (6:1–6). How uncomfortably true it is for us today! Ask any well-known teachers or preachers to compare the reception they get in their own congregation, own town or own country with how they would each be received in other churches, towns or countries. In other places it can be almost embarrassing – the respect nearly borders on reverence – the way people hang onto your words; there are compliments and praise. It is a fresh face, a new voice. They know nothing about the weaknesses of the preacher. They have not yet had time to discover that the preacher has feet of clay, neither do they know the preacher's family or children! Familiarity has had no time to breed contempt.

An expert is a novice away from home.

Similar attitudes to those shown by the people of Nazareth towards Jesus can surface very easily in congregations, small groups and leadership teams within churches. They can occur between marriage partners and within families. It is so easy just to become used to each other, to let another's weaknesses hinder us from appreciating the gifts and strengths of that person. We become prejudiced. We can dismiss another's point of view with the thought 'Oh that is just their idea, I know where they are coming from!' Others sense our lack of encouragement. Sometimes pride gets in the way, competitive attitudes can surface within a leadership team. We can recognise and admire gifts but all too often dismiss them because of some character weakness in the person. Then the gifts and the abilities that God has given do not yield a full harvest.

In short we often shoot ourselves, our leadership team or our congregational activities in the foot. We cripple the potential of our leadership team, our ministry, our congregation by such attitudes and activities.

Overseas speakers or speakers of repute from the bigger cities get high acceptance. We flock to their seminars. We put such people on pedestals, or in the terminology of our last chapter, high up on a ladder of attainment, while locals are cut down to size. So it was for Jesus in Nazareth – the people tried to cut him down to size.

Dare we let this continue to happen in our congregations, in our small groups, in our leadership teams and in our families? Why do we permit prejudice towards each other to disrupt our relationships, create unbelief and restrict the operation of the gifts of God's Spirit among us?

This is not a plea to recognise the gifts of local people in order to stroke their egos, it is a plea to encourage, support and release local giftings so that the blessing of God can be showered on his people. Prejudice and unbelief limit the work of God in the lives of those near to us.

> *'When someone prizes us just as we are,*
> *he or she confirms our existence.'*
> Eugene Kennedy

Style or substance?

We must learn to distinguish between style and substance in a person's ministry. Style is the way they do things, substance is what happens through their ministry. It is all too easy to let something in another's life offend us or put us off. I am not talking about sin or failure but personality differences, style of ministry, slight variations in theological viewpoint or maybe even mannerisms. Comparisons are made, criticisms may be levelled – often most unfairly. Expectancy and faith evaporate; the Holy Spirit is grieved. How discouraging it is for those who have gifts not to be received. What a damper it puts on them and their ministry. That's what happened with the townspeople in Nazareth when Jesus visited. If it happened to Jesus it will most likely happen to us.

The church needs less block and more tackle.

Let us recognise it. When it occurs, let us guard against it. God gifts people in the most marvellous ways. May we not be the reason for those gifts becoming ineffective in the lives of those close to us.

The following story gives us insights as to how we can avoid shooting ourselves in the foot.

A monastery had fallen upon hard times. Once a great order, as a result of waves of anti-monastic persecution in the seventeenth and eighteenth centuries and the rise of secularism in the nineteenth, all its branch houses were lost and it had become decimated to the extent that there were only five monks left in the decaying mother house; the abbot and four others, all over seventy in age. Clearly it was a dying order.

In the deep woods surrounding the monastery there

was a little hut that a rabbi from a nearby town occasionally used for a hermitage. Through their many years
of prayer and contemplation the old monks had become
a bit psychic, so they could always sense when the rabbi
was in his hermitage. 'The rabbi is in the woods, the
rabbi is in the woods again,' they would whisper to each
other. As he agonised over the imminent death of his
order, it occurred to the abbot at one such time to visit
the hermitage and ask the rabbi if by some possible
chance he could offer any advice that might save the
monastery.

The rabbi welcomed the abbot to his hut. But when the
abbot explained the purpose of his visit, the rabbi could
only commiserate with him.

'I know how it is,' he exclaimed. 'The spirit has gone out
of the people. It is the same in my town. Almost no one
comes to the synagogue anymore.' So the old abbot and
the old rabbi wept together. Then they read parts of the
Torah and quietly spoke of deep things.

The time came when the abbot had to leave. They
embraced each other.

'It has been wonderful that we should meet after all
these years,' the old abbot said, 'but I have still failed in
my purpose for coming here. Is there nothing you can
tell me, no piece of advice you can give me that would
help me save my dying order?'

'No I am sorry,' the rabbi responded. 'I have no advice
to give. The only thing I can tell you is that the Messiah
is one of you.'

When the abbot returned to the monastery his fellow
monks gathered around him to ask, 'Well, what did the
rabbi say?'

'He could not help,' the abbot answered. 'We just wept
and read the Torah together. The only thing he did say,
just as I was leaving – it was something cryptic – was
that the Messiah is one of us. I don't know what he
meant.'

In the days and weeks and months that followed, the

old monks pondered this and wondered whether there was any possible significance to the rabbi's words. The Messiah is one of us? Could he possibly have meant one of us here at the monastery? If that's the case, which one? Do you suppose he meant the abbot? Yes, if he meant anyone, he probably meant Father Abbot. He has been our leader for more than a generation. On the other hand, he might have meant Brother Thomas. Certainly Brother Thomas is a holy man. Everyone knows that Thomas is a person of light.

Our beliefs about what we are and what we can be, determine what we will be.

Certainly he could not have meant Brother Elred! Elred gets crotchety at times. But come to think of it, even though he is a thorn in people's sides, when you look back on it, Elred is virtually always right. Often very right. Maybe the rabbi did mean Brother Elred. But surely not Brother Phillip. Phillip is so passive, a real nobody. But then almost mysteriously he has a gift for somehow always being there when you need him. He just magically appears by your side. Maybe Phillip is the Messiah. Of course the rabbi did not mean me. He could not possibly have meant me. I am just an ordinary person, yet supposing he did! Suppose I am the Messiah! O God, not me. I could not be that much for You, could I?

As they contemplated in this manner, the old monks began to treat each other with extraordinary respect on the off chance that one among them might be the Messiah. And on the off chance that each monk himself might be the Messiah, they began to treat themselves with extraordinary respect.

Because the forest in which the monastery was situated was beautiful, it so happened that people still occasionally came to visit it to picnic on its tiny lawn, to wander along some of its paths, even now and then to go into the dilapidated chapel to meditate. As they did so, without even being conscious of it, they sensed this aura of extraordinary respect that now began to surround the five old monks which seemed to radiate out from them and permeate the atmosphere of the place. There was something strangely attractive, even compelling, about it. Hardly knowing why, they began to come back to the monastery more frequently to picnic, to play, to pray. They began to bring their friends to show them this special place. And their friends brought their friends.

Don't just be yourself, be what you ought to be.

Then it happened that some of the younger men who came to visit the monastery started to talk more and more with the old monks. After a while one asked if he could join them. Then another. And another. So within a few years the monastery had once again become a thriving order.

There is no doubt that the way we think about and view each other affects the way we function together. People will only excel if we believe in them. Gifts can only function if we accept them. Ministries will only flourish if we support them. Children will only succeed if we encourage them. Leaders can only rise to the height that people let them. Jesus said, 'Anyone who receives a prophet because he is a prophet will receive a prophet's reward' (Matt 10:41). To recognise, acknowledge and receive gifting, brings reward, blessing and benefit to both the giver and the recipient. That is God's plan and desire for us. May we facilitate his blessing, not restrict it!

Solutions are Humbling

Are you strengthened by your relationship with Christ and do you find comfort from knowing his love? Do you enjoy fellowship with the Holy Spirit and know his kindness and deep sympathy? Then make me happy by living in harmony with each other. Have love for each other and be one in spirit and purpose. Never act from motives of selfish ambition or personal pride, but in humility think more of others than you do of yourself. Each of you must not think only of your own affairs but be concerned about the interests of others. That is – be other-centred not self-centred.

Christ is your example, his attitude should be your attitude. Even though he possessed all the qualities that make God God, he did not cling to the status of what was rightfully his. Of his own free will he stripped himself of all privileges by consenting to be a slave by becoming human. Becoming human, he humbled himself still further by carrying his obedience to death even to die as a common criminal on a cross.

Because of this God has placed him on the highest place and given him a name that is above all other names. At the mention of the name of Jesus every knee in heaven, earth or under the earth will bow and every tongue will openly proclaim that he is Lord, to the glory of God the Father.

(Phil 2:1–11, paraphrased)

So writes a first-century Christian describing the most astonishing event of all eternity.

Servant deity? Preposterous!

Over the centuries scholars have studied the latter part of
this statement (v 6–8) and marvelled at its profoundness. The
more you think about it, the deeper the mystery. Who can
ever plumb its depths or exhaust its meaning and implication? Such a statement sets Christianity apart; unique,
unmatched, proving conclusively that it could never have
been dreamed up by the human mind – even the most bril-
liant, and certainly not two thousand years ago. All cultural
groups know about deity – but servant deity? Impossible!
Servant and deity together, totally incongruous! Deity is
served, not servant. Gods are to be obeyed, not obedient.
They are exalted, not humbled.

> *Thirty-one times in Revelation Jesus is called
> the Lamb – an example of suffering, humility
> and servanthood.*

However, this passage is not just a magnificent theological
declaration full of profound statements, it has important
practical implications. It is not only describing Christ's
motives and attitudes but it is showing us what our motives
and attitudes should be.

The fact is that the approach that Christ took in his relationship with the Father to bring us reconciliation, is the
same approach that we are to take towards others to bring
reconciliation with each other. In these verses we find the
secret of healthy relationships with each other.

It is interesting to reflect on the order of these verses. Paul
starts off this chapter (Phil 2) by talking about our relationships with each other and then seems to use these magnificent statements about Christ's humility as an illustration, or
parenthesis. Having made these statements he then returns
again to a discussion on relationships between Christians in
verses 12–30. Think of it – such an incredible insight just to

illustrate what our relationships with each other should be like! We would have probably made the statements about Christ our primary thrust and then drawn the conclusions.

True humility is not to think too lowly of yourself, but to think rightly and truthfully of yourself.

Consider the relationship-words that precede the statements of verses 6–11 about Christ – being like-minded, having love, being one, not only looking after our own interests, but the interests of others also. Paul says 'this is what I want you to do.' If you really know the love of Christ and the fellowship of the Spirit, then this is what it is all supposed to result in – healthy relationships with each other. Paul's longing for unity between Christians mirrors that of Christ which we looked at earlier.[1] Paul's passion is the same as Christ's passion. Similarly, just as Christ linked us to his Father and himself, in that passionate prayer in the upper room, so now Paul links us to Christ and says, 'If you are going to have right relationships you must have the same attitude as Jesus had.'

Humility essential

So how are these healthy relationships achieved? What is the key that is found here? It is very clear; they come through humility (v 3), through being other-centred (v 4), through serving others (v 7). Nothing is to be done out of selfish ambition or vain conceit, but in humility we should consider others better than ourselves. This is the path to healthy relationships. They are established as we deal with wrong attitudes in our lives.

Christ is our example (v 5). He did not seek to grasp what was rightfully his, to hold onto status and position. He knew who he was and humbly laid it all aside. This is where the devil got it wrong. He was taken up with pride and tried to grasp something that was not rightfully his. He wanted to ascend to be like the Most High. Adam and Eve also got it wrong here, trying to grasp what was not theirs. They wanted to be like God knowing good from evil. However Jesus released what was rightfully his; he became a servant and humbled himself to obey. That is really what humility is – it is obedience. To voluntarily place one's life under the control of another, to obey what they say – that is humility.

Consider the steps Jesus took;
- as God he became human,
- as a human he becomes a servant,
- as servant he becomes a slave, and
- as a slave he dies.

All humble steps of obedience to his Father.

Pride is like rust, it corrodes the soul.

There are two keys words when it comes to establishing healthy relationships. In a nutshell they describe the life of Christ. These two words should become an integral part of our lives. They are humility and servanthood – not popular words in today's self-centred, individualistic, competitive society, but nevertheless biblical words, words that apply to the one we follow and he intends that these should apply to his followers. These two words need to be written on the minds and consciences of every Christian.

Listen to the words of Jesus, 'Come to me, all you who are weary and burdened, and I will give you rest. Take my yoke upon you and learn from me, for I am gentle and humble in heart, and you will find rest for your souls. For my yoke is easy and my burden is light' (Matt 11:28–30). 'Weary and burdened?' says Jesus. 'Then learn from me. Take my yoke, be linked to me, do it my way and gentleness and humility will bring rest to your souls.' True, isn't it. Think of all that nervous and emotional energy we expend in fighting for our own rights, attempting to climb the ladder of success, trying to create an impression, striving to attain position, handling the pressures of competitiveness, or seeking to dominate in relationships. Jesus offers rest for our souls. It is only in fellowship with him that such rest is attained, as we 'yoke', or link, our life to his.

Servanthood leads to greatness

Listen again to Jesus as he says, 'Whoever wants to become great among you must be your servant, and whoever wants to be first must be your slave — just as the Son of Man did not come to be served, but to serve, and to give his life as a ransom for many' (Matt 20:26–28). Being a servant is the key to true greatness in the kingdom of God. This was not the view of society in Jesus' day. Servants were at the bottom of that pecking order. Neither is it the view of our society today, but then the values of the kingdom of God are often in sharp contrast to the values of the kingdom of this world.

One of Christ's most astonishing, humble, servant activities on earth was that of washing his disciples' feet. We read, 'Knowing that he had come from God and was returning to God . . . he [took] a towel . . .' (Jn 13:3–4). Here is true humility. He knew who he was – 'He had come from God and was returning to God.' He did not have an inflated opinion of himself, nor did he have a low opinion of himself. This true humility enabled him to take a towel and wash his disciples' feet. Not only was this a statement about humility and servant attitudes, it was also a statement about youth and women. Only girl slaves washed people's feet. There were few lower jobs that he could have chosen to show his servant-heart. By this one humble act he modelled for us the path to successful relationship and brought dignity to both women and youth.

> *'The service we render to others is really the rent we*
> *pay for our room on this earth. It is obvious that*
> *people are travellers; that the purpose of this world*
> *is not "to have and to hold" but "to give and serve".*
> *There can be no other meaning.'*
> *Sir Wilfred T. Grenfell*

During my teenage years I had a friend who, whenever there was a dirty job to be done or someone was asked to do some cleaning around the church, would be the first to volunteer. For a teenager this was somewhat unusual and was a matter of comment among many people in the congregation. It was of little surprise to many of us that God took him onto the mission field and into a pioneering work. He had learned to serve and you can trust a person who has learned to serve.

Biblical humility

Show me a relationship problem and I will show you a lack of humility. Show me a relationship problem and I will show you people who have not learned how to serve each other. Show me a relationship problem and somewhere you will find pride raising its head. Show me a relationship problem and I will show you rights being emphasised rather than responsibilities. Maybe if more humility and servant attitudes were encouraged between protagonists in the counselling rooms of our nations there would be a much greater chance of success in healing the fractured relationships all around us. All too often when relationships are strained, pride surfaces, rights are demanded, people seek to enforce their will and have their way in situations.

Biblical humility means thinking truthfully about ourselves.

Biblical humility means being able to lay aside what is rightfully ours.

Biblical humility means having a sane assessment of our gifts and abilities.

Biblical humility means being obedient.

Biblical humility means thinking of others as better than ourselves.

Biblical humility means accepting my responsibilities rather than demanding my rights.

Biblical humility means being on the plane, not placing ourselves on some scale of attainment or comparison with others.

Biblical humility means laying down our lives for others.

Biblical humility means setting aside self-interest.

Biblical humility means discarding independence and individualism.

Biblical humility means rejecting status.

'Unity is corporate humility.'
Dean Sherman

In both the Old and New Testaments God constantly comes alongside the humble but comes against the proud. God hates pride but responds quickly to humility. Pride brings God's judgment, but humility brings God's blessing.

One of the human characteristics evidenced most clearly in the last days will be pride. In 2 Timothy 3:1–4 we read,

> But mark this: There will be terrible times in the last days. People will be lovers of themselves, lovers of money, **boastful**, **proud**, abusive, disobedient to their parents, ungrateful, unholy, without love, unforgiving, slanderous, without self-control, brutal, not lovers of the good, treacherous, rash, **conceited**, lovers of pleasure rather than lovers of God.

Three separate Greek words are used here to describe various forms of pride, they are translated as 'boastful', 'proud' and 'conceited'. It is almost as if the writer is saying, 'Beware, pride will be a special problem in the last days.'

The people of Israel are often accused of being stiff-necked – another way of expressing pride, and God rebukes them, punishes them or humbles them. In Deuteronomy 8:2–3 we read that God had to humble them in the desert because they refused to go into the land he had promised. Pride seems to inevitably bring disaster on people in the Old Testament.

> *One way to restore humility is to read the help-wanted ads. You will be surprised how many positions there are which you are too ignorant, too unattractive or too old to fill.*

Consider the following events as people either humbled themselves or refused to humble themselves:

- Ahab did, at one stage, and prevented a disaster coming on the nation of Israel (1 Ki 21:29).
- Belshazzar knew better, but did not and lost his king-

dom to the Medes and Persians (Dan 5:22).
- Rehoboam and the leaders of Israel did and God sent deliverance to them (2 Chron 12:6–7).
- Zedekiah did not and so the people of Israel were carried off into captivity (2 Chron 36:11–13).
- Hezekiah did and God's anger did not come upon him or the people of Israel (2 Chron 32:26).
- Pharaoh did not, so plagues came on the land of Egypt (Ex 10:3–4).
- Manasseh, a very corrupt monarch, did once and God brought him back to his kingdom (2 Chron 33:12–13).
- Judah did not, so God brought disaster on them (Jer 44:10–11).
- Josiah did and God promised that the evil planned for Judah would not occur while he lived (2 Chron 34:27–28).
- Whenever Israel did, God promised he would respond to them (Lev 26:40–42).

Pride coming before a fall, is well documented in the history of God's people, and reminds me of the following illustration.

> *It is possible to be too big for God to use you*
> *but never too small for God to use you.*

In a certain pond on a farm were two ducks and a frog. These neighbours were the best of friends. All day long they used to play together. As the hot summer days came, the pond began to dry up and soon there was so little water left that they all realised that they would have to move. The ducks could easily fly to another place, but what about their friend the frog?

Finally the ducks decided that they would hold a stick between them in their bills. The frog could hang onto the stick with his mouth and they would fly him to another pond. This is what they did. As they were flying along with the frog between them clutching the stick with his mouth, a farmer out in his field looked up and saw them and said,

'Well, isn't that a clever idea I wonder who thought of it!'

To which the frog replied, 'I did . . .'!

There are many other references in both Old and New Testament where the importance of humility is emphasised.[2] Paul constantly talks of himself as a servant, first of Christ, and also of others.

One of the privileges of being in pastoral work is that of officiating at the marriages of young people within the congregation. I remember clearly one such couple, Sally and Eric.[3] They were older than most and their developing friendship had been a great joy to see. As with all couples embarking on marriage there was a certain degree of trepidation for those of us looking on. With the pressures in marriage today one cannot help but wonder how each marriage will turn out. One of the added concerns in this case was that this couple were from different cultural backgrounds. Such a union brings extra, but not insurmountable pressures. I was delighted to be approached to officiate at the wedding. Our practice is to encourage those being married to plan their own wedding. Theirs was a very different event, full of joy, spontaneous participation, laughter, very moving and a marvellous blend of both cultures. Neither Eric nor Sally prepared or memorised set vows – they ad libbed on the day – not a procedure that I would normally recommend, but one that was most appropriate for them and full of significance. When I asked for the rings they could not be found, the best man had hidden them. When he went to get them from where he had placed them they were not there, someone else had subsequently re-hidden them! You can imagine the consternation and relaxed good humour.

Did you ever notice that the sweetest music comes from the smallest birds?

And so a memorable day passed. However, within a few months the marriage had come under great pressure. When Eric became frustrated and then angry the couple temporarily parted for some space. This parting inevitably became known within the congregation and many people were concerned and saddened. People experienced in marriage counselling became involved and sought to resolve issues that had surfaced, seeking to bring reconciliation between the partners. Things were very delicate; it was touch-and-go as to whether the marriage would survive. Many people were praying. After some weeks of reflection, counselling and discussions, Sally and Eric came to a position of recommitment to their marriage and decided to resume living together. At this stage several of us felt that some form of public recommitment was necessary. The recent events had become quite widely known. They were a high-profile couple and so we felt there needed to be some form of public reaffirmation. With a degree of apprehension I approached them and asked them to consider the following suggestion. I felt that 1 Peter 5:5–6 ('Clothe yourselves with humility towards one another, because, "God opposes the proud but gives grace to the humble". Humble yourselves, therefore, under God's mighty hand, that he may lift you up in due time') was particularly appropriate and shared this with them. They thought it over for a few days and came back to me with a definite 'Yes' they would do it. On the next Sunday in front of many people in our congregation, they humbly acknowledged their failures of recent weeks. They admitted that what had come between them was wrong. They shed tears (so did others in the congregation) and many of their friends gathered round them to pray for them.

> *God's re-creation is more difficult than his original creation because it depends on flawed individuals.*

Eric and Sally's marriage has been strong, not perfect, from that day as I write seven years after the event. I believe this incident illustrates several principles that need to be kept in mind regarding relationships.

- Humility always brings God's grace and blessing. The public acknowledgment of mistakes was a very humbling step to take. It was far from easy but resulted in God's blessing. Humility always brings God's response.

God pours his grace upon the humble. The humility of Christ led to his exaltation (Phil 2:9).

- Confession of faults to each other brings forgiveness and healing (Jas 5:16).
- By public acknowledgment, gossip and misunderstanding are prevented from escalating.
- Public acknowledgment of failure or need draws from other people a great deal of empathy and support.
- When an event such as this becomes public knowledge, it needs to be corrected publicly.

The two ideas of humility and servanthood are simple ideas but their implementation may be a different matter. I would not be so naive as to suggest that humility and servant attitudes are easy to attain. Nor am I suggesting that this is all that is needed to sort out strained relationships. However, Scripture seems to make it abundantly clear that they are foundational for healthy human relationships. Without them, relationships will most certainly flounder.

> *'Success and humility make good partners in your*
> *life. Allow them to complement each other.'*
> *Thomas A. Brown*

Humility – a choice

I believe we can choose humility and we can adopt a servant attitude. These are choices that we can make. They are pathways that we can decide to follow. Unfortunately all too often we reject them and choose attitudes that are self-centred. Pride is a very corrupting force and many times we are not aware that this is what is motivating us. Normally God does not create humility in us – we are told to 'humble ourselves'.

I can choose to make the following statements, humbly acknowledging my wrong actions or attitudes towards someone with whom I have a relationship problem:

'I was wrong.'   'I am sorry.'   'Please forgive me.'

'I forgive you.'   'Can I help you?'   'Could you help me?'
'I apologise for . . .'

Some Christians expect God to do something miraculous when relationship situations are bad, when often the genuine use of such statements can be a great step forward. When it comes to the development and restoration of relationships there are no easy solutions or instant answers. This is not good news in an age of quick-fix remedies.

> *God has two thrones, one in the highest heaven*
> *and the other in the lowest heart.*

God's intention is to re-create us into the likeness of his Son. God's re-creation is more difficult than his original creation because it depends on flawed individuals. He has given us resources to live our Christian faith; we need to use these if we are to grow in our relationships together. There are four key resources:

A. The cross

The cross deals with three areas of broken relationships. Because of the cross –

Forgiveness is possible for broken relationships.
Healing is available for past hurts.
Our self-centred, sinful nature has been dealt with.

All of the wrong attitudes that spoil relationships spring from our sinful nature. Spoiled relationships are the fruit of a root, that root is sin. Galatians 5:19–26 says,

The acts of the sinful nature are obvious: sexual immorality, impurity and debauchery; idolatry and witchcraft; hatred, discord, jealousy, fits of rage, selfish ambition, dissensions, factions and envy; drunkenness, orgies, and the like. I warn you, as I did before, that those who live like this will not inherit the kingdom of

God.

But the fruit of the Spirit is love, joy, peace, patience, kindness, goodness, faithfulness, gentleness and self-control. Against such things there is no law. Those who belong to Christ Jesus have crucified the sinful nature with its passions and desires. Since we live by the Spirit, let us keep in step with the Spirit. Let us not become conceited, provoking and envying each other.

Notice how many acts of the sinful nature are relationship-based; hatred, discord, jealousy, rage, selfish ambition, dissensions, factions. We are to crucify the old nature and live in the Spirit. Ephesians 4:22–24 tells us to 'put off your old self, which is being corrupted by its deceitful desires; to be made new in the attitude of your minds; and to put on the new self, created to be like God in true righteousness and holiness'.

The New Testament paints the picture of our old nature and new nature as being implacable enemies. Galatians 5:17 tells us that 'the sinful nature desires what is contrary to the Spirit, and the Spirit what is contrary to the sinful nature. They are in conflict with each other, so that you do not do what you want.' The remedy is to put to death the old nature and live in the new nature – the Spirit. These actions are two sides of the same coin. For those of us brought up in conservative evangelical churches we have heard a lot about the putting to death of the old nature – the cross (Rom 6) but not much about living in the Spirit (Rom 8). For those in charismatic or Pentecostal circles, the emphasis has been on living in the Spirit (Rom 8), while the on-going work of the cross (Rom 6) has often been overlooked. I have attended many charismatic and Pentecostal churches, conferences and seminars but have very seldom heard teaching on the cross in the life of the Christian (Rom 6). We need to apply both aspects when it comes to right relationships and living in holiness; one without the other is not the full gospel. The cross for the Christian means 'your good at my expense'.

Self-denial or self-fulfilment?

For the last twenty years the church has followed the world and emphasised self-fulfilment in Christ rather than self-denial with Christ. 'I' is the central letter of pride and sin and is the letter placed first in 'individualism' and 'independence'. We come to Christ for health and wealth and do not like to hear about death or self-denial. Such teaching is not very popular, it does not draw the crowds, it is not exciting. I fear that much of the hype and excitement that forms the basis of many congregations today may be deadening our hearts and minds to these truths. We are reaping a sad harvest, the fall out rate from such situations is considerable. Jesus made it very clear that for seeds to multiply they must first die.

Are we self-centred?
If you are in a photo who do you look at first?

For many years I struggled with what it meant to crucify the old life. Then one day as I was praying about it, I stumbled on a key. We crucify the old nature when we choose the opposite to what we would naturally do. By nature we are more likely to choose what is wrong, to get angry in situations or with people, to be jealous, proud or competitive. Despite the fact that we are capable of much that is good, our bias is towards sin and towards our own self-centredness. Most people would not choose to be crucified, it is no doubt an extremely unpleasant experience. Choosing to crucify our old life is not easy or pleasant either, that is why we tend to ignore this aspect of our Christian life. It hurts. It hurts to apologise, to put things right with my Christian brother or sister. It hurts to face my mistakes and weakness. It hurts to deal with my self-centredness and individualism. It hurts to choose the opposite to the way I would naturally go. But what is it that gets hurt? Isn't it so often our pride? Well, is that necessarily a bad thing?

An old monk used to give this piece of advice to his novices:

Remember the paradox:
To live you have to die.
Give and you will receive.
Lose and you will find.
Obey and you will be free.

There is a lot of truth wrapped up in those few lines. They may seem so contrary to all that our media promotes, or our society advocates. However, the kingdom that we belong to is the upside-down kingdom, so we should not be surprised at such an apparent paradox.

B. The Spirit

The second resource God has given us for healthy relationships is his Spirit. As was pointed out above, walking in the Spirit is the other half of the 'crucifying of the old life' equation. How deadly the Christian life would be if all we could do was go around all day seeking to crucify the old life.

It is the Spirit who brings vitality, refreshment, comfort and support. It is the Spirit who reveals sin in our lives, not to condemn but to establish humility. It is the Spirit who will produce the fruit in our lives. It is the Spirit who brings new life. It is the Spirit who re-sensitises our conscience. I have never ceased to be amazed at how a new Christian's conscience suddenly 'lights up' after they come to know God. Things that in their former life they never even thought about now suddenly cause them concern. Without the Spirit there is no Christian life.

Strong relationship with God leads to strong relationships with each other. True intimacy with God enhances intimacy with others. Genuine humility before God encourages humility before others. The closer we get to the Lord, the closer we get to others.

Much of our growth as Christians involves learning to be led and to walk in the Spirit. It is as if we have been placed in a new environment and we have to learn everything from scratch. I have observed that the filling of the Spirit releases the power of God and his gifts in our lives, but not the fruit. Fruit takes time, it takes co-operation with the Holy Spirit.

> *Of the seven churches in Revelation, five needed*
> *renewal after only sixty years of church history.*

In our lives we should always apply the cross (dead to the old) and the Spirit (alive in the new). The cross cuts out, while the Spirit adds.

We need to pray that God will move mightily by his Spirit in our congregations, our leadership teams and small groups. Renewing and refreshing movements of the Holy Spirit are almost always characterised by a deepening and strengthening of human relationships. One of Jonathan Edwards' five tests to determine a genuine work of the Holy Spirit is that it will produce a greater love for God and people. Renewal and refreshing movements of the Holy Spirit have been marked by a strengthening of loving relationships between people. The Spirit truly does bring unity.

C. The Word

The third resource God has given us for healthy relationships is his Word. God's Word, the Bible, is the foundation on which we build our lives. As we read it, meditate on it and pray it in, it purifies our thoughts and lives. It is a guideline for us. It brings the eternal, constant truths of God to us amidst a world of transience and relativity. It probes our motives. It is food to our soul. It brings comfort and hope. It is here that we hear the words of Christ and start to understand God's purposes. It is here that we learn about ourselves, our potential in God and the problems that beset us. It illuminates our pathway in life. Sometimes it is like a sword piercing our lives. I acknowledge the challenge that this chapter has brought to me as I have been reflecting on the Scriptures. The psalmist could say, 'Thy word have I hid in my heart that I might not sin against thee.' This includes the sin of broken and strained relationships. Regular reflection and meditation on God's Word will help strengthen and develop our relationships

D. Prayer

The fourth resource God has given us for healthy relationships is prayer. If God's Word is food to the Christian, then prayer must be the Christian's breath.

This is not the place to explore the whole topic of prayer. Many have done it and there are well-known masterpieces on prayer in Christian literature. Communion with the Father was central in the life of Christ. What strength he must have gathered from his hours in prayer; often out in solitary places, sometimes praying all night. Of all the resources that we have been given, prayer would have to be the most neglected. What percentage of people attend a prayer meeting in your congregation? I wonder if the lack of prayer together is an indication of a lack of prayer individually. If it is, then we are guilty of abusing a privilege – I speak to myself.

> *There is nothing that causes us to love people so much as praying for them.*

Pray for friends, enemies and everyone in between

Jesus said that we should 'pray for those who persecute us' (Matt 5:44). He did this himself as he hung on the cross and asked the Father to forgive those who had put him there. If we are urged to pray for those who persecute us then I guess we should be praying for those with whom we are experiencing tense or difficult relationships. We need to pray for their blessing. In Luke 6:28 we read 'Bless those who curse you, pray for those who ill-treat you.' I have regularly encouraged people whom I have counselled in the area of relationship struggles, to pray for the blessing of the other party. It is often said that prayer changes things and this is true. However, prayer also changes people – the pray-er. It is quite amazing to see what can happen in us when we pray for God's blessing on a person or group with whom we are experiencing difficult relationships. Unfortunately when we get into difficult relationships it is much easier to criticise, to defend ourselves, to hold grudges, or to be unforgiving. All these attitudes arise from our sinful nature not the Spirit of God.

Why criticise when we can pray?

The Apostle Paul cultivated the same attitudes in his life when he faced people opposing him. He said, 'when we are cursed, we bless . . . when we are slandered, we answer kindly' (1 Cor 4:12) and again he says, 'Bless those who persecute you, bless and do not curse' (Rom 12:14). There are some things that we must learn to accept. There are some things that we cannot change. Maybe there are relationship situations that we can go no further with, we have done all that is humanly possible. Then we must just accept them. This is not a popular solution in an age that emphasises my rights, but it is a way that both Jesus and Paul advocated. Much of Paul's suffering resulted from difficult relationships (2 Cor 11:23–33) but he had learnt to rest in the grace of God (2 Cor 12:9). He could say, 'When we are cursed, we bless; when we are persecuted, we endure it; when we are slandered, we answer kindly. Up to this moment we have become the scum of the earth, the refuse of the world' (1 Cor 4:12–13). The same was true of Jesus, Peter writes, 'When they hurled their insults at him, he did not retaliate; when he suffered, he made no threats. Instead, he entrusted himself to him who judges justly' (1 Pet 2:23).

Creation groans. We groan. God groans.
(Rom 8:22,23,26)

Some things we cannot change, it is then that we need to be changed or we will become angry and bitter. Praying for those who oppose us deals with the attitudes that rise in our hearts. Why should we let another person's wrong doing cause us to do wrong as well?

The Holy Spirit also prays
One final thought about prayer – the Holy Spirit also prays

for us (Rom 8:26). It is particularly significant that this statement comes at the end of a discussion about sufferings. We
read that God's creation has been frustrated by sin, that the
whole of creation is groaning, waiting for us, the children of
God, to be released into all that God has for us in a coming
day. That we, who have the firstfruits of the Spirit, are also
groaning waiting for redemption. What is causing creation to
groan? What are we groaning about? Well, in what ways has
sin spoiled the whole of God's creation? Several ways could
be listed, but surely one of the main ones would have to be
in that area of relationships. Sin has distorted people's relationship with God, with each other and with creation itself.
So what is the Holy Spirit interceding about? Is it too much
to presume that at least part of his intercession on our behalf
is for strained or broken relationships between people? Does
the Trinity still feel the heartache of broken human relationships? Does the intercession of the Holy Spirit match that
passionate prayer of Jesus in the upper room? Is he praying
for the same things; unity, love between people, oneness,
deep relationship? We cannot be one hundred per cent sure
of the answers to these questions. Sometimes Scripture is
tantalisingly brief on topics. We know very little about the
content of the prayers of Christ and here we do not know the
content of the prayer ministry of the Holy Spirit. We do
know that the Holy Spirit searches our hearts and intercedes
for us in accordance with God's will (Rom 8:27). If God's will
is restored relationships, surely then the Holy Spirit is interceding about these.

What a profound significance this places on the topic that
we are discussing in this book. Jesus and the Holy Spirit both
interceding about our relationships as people. What a high
priority we should place on this topic, how we should be
guarding and growing in our relationships with others.

Interpreting motives? Dangerous!

How easy it is for little things to spoil relationships. We can go backwards five paces in an instant. These five paces may then take us months to recover. I am always amazed at how easy it is to misread someone's actions and completely misunderstand that person. I sometimes find myself jumping to conclusions about situations, only to later discover that I had come to completely the wrong conclusions. If I had acted on them how disastrous the results would have been. It is a truism 'that anything that can be misunderstood will be misunderstood'. What a powerful effect misunderstandings have on relationships. I remember a member of our congregation phoning me one day. The call went something like this –

'Brian, have you got something against me?'

'No Val! Why do you say that?'

'Well, when you came into the building before the service started last Sunday, you looked straight at me and didn't even acknowledge my presence. So I thought that you must be holding something against me?'

> *'Do not be disturbed at being not understood:*
> *be disturbed rather at not being understanding.'*
> *Chinese proverb*

I had to think quickly. I could not even remember seeing her at the commencement of the service, let alone purposely failing to acknowledge her. Then I remembered what I had been doing. I had come to the service and was urgently needing to speak to our worship leader before the service. What I had been doing was scanning the people who had arrived trying to find him. No doubt as I had been doing this I had momentarily looked at the woman now on the other end of the telephone without any recognition. Val had taken this as a slight on my part and had been worrying about it for several days. She had seen my actions and jumped to conclusions about my motives. Her reasoning was – 'Brian did that – this must be the reason why he did it.' She had seen an action and jumped to a wrong conclusion about a motive. I was quickly

able to put the record straight and we hung up our telephones on good terms. I was glad that at least she had had
the courage to confront the issue and get it sorted out. So
often we just assume things and jump to damaging and
wrong conclusions about people's motives. It is often difficult enough sorting out our own motives let alone trying to
determine another person's, yet we so often find ourselves
doing it. God is the only one who knows motives and he will
expose these in a coming day (1 Cor 4:5).

I am reminded of the story of the young man who loved
driving. He had a beautiful, fast red sports car. He loved to
drive on country roads and thought of himself as a great
driver – he could handle anything. One day he was out driving along his favourite road and coming into his favourite
curve was a car careening out of control. Just before it got to
him it pulled out of his lane. As it went past the woman driver yelled out, 'Pig!'

He shot back, 'Cow!'

'How dare she call me a name,' he thought, 'I was in my
lane she was the one all over the road.' He felt especially
pleased that he had managed to shout at her as she went
past. He put his foot to the floor, whipped around the curve
and ran into a pig!

Assuming another's motives for their actions often puts us
on very shaky ground.

It was said of Jesus that,

> He will delight in the fear of the LORD.
> He will not judge by what he sees with his eyes,
>   or decide by what he hears with his ears;
> but with righteousness he will judge the needy,
>   with justice he will give decisions for the poor of the
>   earth. . . .
> Righteousness will be his belt
>   and faithfulness the sash around his waist.

(Is 11:3–5).

His discernment in situations would always be with justice,
righteousness and faithfulness, it would not be just by sight

and hearing. When it comes to our relationships with each other, there is a very important lesson here for us.

Someone has said that life is 10 per cent what happens to you and 90 per cent how you react. The question is, will our reaction be self-centred or servant-hearted? Will it be out of pride or humility? The choices are ours.

RESOURCES AND RELATIONSHIPS

I was talking about money and materialism to an audience of university students. As I held up a ten dollar note from which I had just cut off a one sq cm corner I was explaining that this one sq cm was equivalent to the eighteen cents given to God from every ten dollars that all Christians from around the world earn.

'In terms of the kingdom of God, where does the rest of this money go?' I asked the audience. There were a few murmured responses.

'Well, most of it is non-productive and is wasted in terms of God's kingdom,' I continued, and to illustrate the point I proceeded to set fire to the remaining part of the ten dollar bill. The response of the students was most interesting. Some were nearly frantic as they saw the ten dollars consumed by the flame. Others gasped with astonishment – not at the illustration but at the destruction of the ten dollars. For some, it was all they could do to sit still and stop themselves rushing up to rescue the bill – after all they were students!

Money will buy a fine dog, but only love
will cause it to wag its tail.

Money is powerful stuff! People will go to extraordinary lengths to obtain it, protect it and keep it. They will scheme and plan as to how they can get more of it. They will destroy relationships for it. They will work long hours and cripple family life for it. They will steal and kill for it. They will risk life and limb for it. They will be driven to an early grave because of it. They will make huge sacrifices to gain more of it. They will admire the pile of it that they have accumulated and they will never think that they have enough of it. Little wonder then that Jesus said so much about it.

You can't take your money to heaven but you can send it on ahead.

It is impossible to talk about relationships between people in congregations without talking about how we utilise our material resources for each other's benefit. Biblical relationships are not just spiritual, emotional or friendship bonds they also have economic implications. In this chapter we will be looking more at 'economics' than 'giving'. By teaching only on 'giving', the Church has had far too narrow a view of God's perspective on money and possessions. Many lifestyles of Christians indicate that their understanding of this topic can be summarised by the statement, 'So long as I give God his bit, the rest is mine to use as I please.' Biblical economics paints a much bigger picture of the use of our resources.

Biblical economics can be defined as the way God intends his people to utilise the finite resources that he has given them. It is summarised in one word – stewardship.

The two greatest problem areas in our society would have to be the breakdown in human relationships and the hold that materialism has over people's lives. Both are inextricably bound together and affect each other. Both occupy a considerable amount of space in the biblical record. Both offer huge potential for Christians to demonstrate something uniquely different to the society around them. These two areas would also be the biggest areas of struggle in our Christian lives. Often our greatest struggles present the greatest opportunities.

When people cease to worship God they begin to worship other gods.

*Israel left the worship of God for the worship of
Baal (leading to impurity), Moloch (leading to cruel-
ty), and Mammon (leading to the lust of possessions).
During the twentieth century modern humanity has
prostrated itself before the same three gods.*

Recently I have come to see three basic biblical principles
that are very clearly linked –

1. How we handle our relationships is a measure of our
    maturity in God. It is the main test of our Christian
    maturity.
2. How we handle our physical resources is a measure of
    our **faithfulness** (trustworthiness) to God. Luke 16:11
    says 'If you have not been trustworthy in handling
    worldly wealth, who will trust you with true riches?'
3. Our **effectiveness** and ministry in the kingdom of God
    is directly related to our faithfulness, not our gifted-
    ness. We can be very gifted (tongues, prophecy,
    knowledge, faith) and very sacrificial (give to the poor,
    give our body to be burned), but if love is lacking then
    giftedness and sacrifice are worth nothing (1 Cor 13:13).

Giftedness is a measure of God's grace towards us.
Trustworthiness is our gift to God. God has given us something very practical and tangible as a test of how trustworthy
we are – this is our material resources. Material resources are
visible, within our grasp and control. They are not hard to
measure, intangible qualities. He assesses trustworthiness by
something very practical, how we use these material
resources.

There is a very significant scripture that links both relationships and resources,

This is how we know what love is: Jesus Christ laid
down his life for us. And we ought to lay down our
lives for our brothers. If anyone has material possessions and sees his brother in need but has no pity on

him, how can the love of God be in him? Dear children, let us not love with words or tongue but with actions and in truth.

(1 Jn 3:16)

Success in life has nothing to do with what you gain in life or accomplish for yourself. It's what you do for others.

John makes the following points in these verses:

- Love means laying down our lives for others – a very other-centred activity.
- Laying down our lives means using our possessions for others.
- Using our possessions for others is love in action.

Let me summarise this linkage:

1. Mature relationships (love)

Means

2. Using our resources for others

Indicates

3. Our faithfulness to God

Enhances

4. Our effectiveness in the kingdom of God

John's first epistle is a letter about relationships. Relationship with God and relationship with others. In a nutshell John says that true relationships (love) demand that we use our resources for others. How does this link with laying down my life for others? We can look at it this way, I use time to earn income. Time is something I cannot get back so in effect it is 'spent' and represents part of my earthly life which I lay down. Therefore I am laying down my life when I use my money or possessions for others. Jesus said, 'Greater love has no man than this, that a man lay down his life for his friends.'

We should not be surprised at this close linkage between our resources and our relationships. It is a major theme throughout the Bible which we will now consider.

It has often been noted that starting points are significant events in the biblical record. This is why Genesis so often forms an essential book to study in any Bible study course. Starting points show us God's initial intention. We see what is on his heart. It is at starting points that we get clear insights into the kingdom of God.

> ***Wealth consists not in having many possessions
> but in having few wants.***

There seem to be at least five key starting points in Scripture;

1. The creation narrative.
2. The formation of the nation of Israel.
3. The life of Jesus.
4. The New Testament church.
5. The coming kingdom when Christ returns.

At each of these points principles involving the economic relationships between the people of God's kingdom are laid out. We will now examine these.

Starting point 1: Creation principles

Without going into great detail and explanation, here are some of the major economic principles that we can discover in the first two chapters of Genesis.

a) God is the creator of everything and therefore the ultimate owner of all.

b) People are part of God's creation. Human beings have

no absolute ownership of the rest of God's creation.

c) God has given the earth to people to manage – the principle of stewardship.

d) There is an expectation of growth. God says, 'be fruitful and increase' (Gen 1:28). One can assume that economic growth is also part of this mandate as well as reproductive productivity.

e) Exploitation was not God's intention for this planet.

f) Every person should have equal access to the resources of God's creation.

Physical resources, people and God are clearly intertwined. We relate to God as owner of all we possess. We relate to our resources as stewards and we relate to others around us as fellow recipients of God's goodness and grace, sharers together of God's physical resources.

> *Snobbery – spending money you do not have,*
> *to buy things you do not need,*
> *to impress people you do not like.*

Starting point 2: The formation of the Jewish nation

It is particularly to the book of Deuteronomy that we turn to learn about the economic principles given to the nation of Israel. Here it is very important that we discover the principles which lie behind the economic practices that Moses outlined to Israel. The practices outlined for the nation as they were about to enter their own land for the first time may not be appropriate in the twentieth century. However there will be principles that we need to discover and consider how we could apply in our modern world.

Israel had come out of four hundred years of slavery. Their understanding of economic principles would have been at best limited. It was therefore essential that God should outline his principles for them as they stood on the border of their land. Here is a summary of some of them.

a)   God owned the land and he was gifting it to Israel to steward. A similar understanding to that found in the creation principles.

b)   The land was not divided into equal shares but in such a way so as everybody had enough.

c)   Land was to be returned to its owners in the fiftieth year, clearly a mechanism to prevent poor people becoming poorer and the rich becoming richer at the poor's expense.

d)   Boundary stones, indicating the extent of people's land, were not to be moved. Punishment for movement of boundary stones was the same as punishment for idolatry, adultery, murder. God is utterly opposed to dishonest economic practices.

It's impossible to save money when your neighbours keep on buying things you cannot afford.

e)   The land owner was to leave grain standing at the edges of the field and those reaping the crops had to leave handfuls behind them so that the poor people could then come and gather for their own food. This is the gleaning principle. Those with surplus must share with those in need, but the needy are expected to contribute to the gathering of their own food – it is not just to be a hand-out.

f)   The first fruits of crops had to be offered to God. This reminded the people that their economic productivity originated with God.

g)   Slaves had to be allowed to go free and all debts were to be cancelled every seventh year. Further principles to prevent the poor getting poorer and the rich getting richer at their expense that God wanted his people to build into their economic structures (Deut 15:3–4).

h)   There was to be one day in seven and one year in seven for rest for people, slaves and animals. Rest and relaxation are an essential part of the economy of God.

i)   If a Jew gave his coat as a guarantee for a loan, the

lender had to give it back overnight. In God's eyes a person's health and well-being were of greater importance than the security of another's money. Whisper that in the ear of your bank manager tomorrow!

j)   Wages had to be paid at the end of each day. This would ensure that people always had money to cover necessities

k)   No interest was to be charged on money loaned to fellow Israelites. A further guideline to prevent people from profiting from the misfortune of others.

Materialism is not the answer to the meaning of life.
It's unsatisfying and there are not enough resources
to go around.

l)   Several times we hear God reminding his people that they had been slaves, 'Remember that you were slaves.' God was saying, 'You know what it was like to be slaves. Never treat others in the same way as you have been treated.'

m)   God's intention was that Israel should enjoy the fruit of their labours (Deut 8:10) and productivity was his intention for his people (Deut 16:15).

Clearly God intended to prevent his people from sliding into debt, poverty and bondage. These practices with their underlying principles were unheard of in other nations of that day. In the nations around Israel it was dog eat dog. Such practices involved a clear understanding of the fact that God's resources were for everybody to share. Those who had surplus were constantly reminded of their responsibility towards others less well off.

Economic growth and productivity were expected. The question is to what end would the productivity be put. The benefits of that growth had to be made available to all of Israel. Two of the underlying principles of Old Testament economics would have to be – no greed, no covetousness. Greed – having more than I need. Covetousness – wanting what I don't need.

Again we see the close connection between resources and human relationships that God intended for his people Israel.

Starting point 3: The life and teaching of Jesus

The overarching theme of the teaching of Jesus is the kingdom of God. However the topic that he talked about the most was resources – money and material possessions. He talked about money almost 100 times in Matthew, and one third of the parables and one verse in every seven in Luke speak about material possessions. There are 500 references in the New Testament to prayer but 1,000 to a person's relationship to his or her possessions.

> *The addiction to materialism is fed every hour of every day in this society. It is not only legal to feed that addiction, it is the whole purpose of the system. It is our reason for being – to possess and consume.*

Jesus indicates that possessions are a great resource for his kingdom if they are released, but strangle the spiritual life out of people if they are hoarded. Stewardship of material resources is the theme of many parables and stewardship means that we cannot do whatever we like with what we own. A steward simply manages goods for another, thus a Christian view of possession is that they belong to God and we manage them on his behalf. Jesus even collected up food after feeding the 5,000, thus modelling good stewardship.

God has given physical resources to people to develop their character, gifts and abilities. Good management of these resources means greater effectiveness in God's kingdom both now and in the future.

When it comes to money and material possessions Jesus is very critical of selfishness. He is consistently negative about accumulated wealth and tells several parables where those who used wealth only for themselves are seen in a very disparaging light. He says it is pointless to gain the whole world and yet lose one's soul (Lk 9:25). The rich man, who apparently ignored Lazarus at his gate, is told that while he had good things in life and Lazarus had bad things, those roles were now reversed (Lk 16:19–31). The rich man who builds bigger barns to store more for himself but then dies is called a fool (Lk 12:16–21). Jesus told a parable about a wedding banquet and guests that were more concerned about their material possessions than coming to the wedding of a friend (Matt 22:1–14). He called those who did not feed the hungry, give clothing or accommodation to the needy, 'goats', saying they will be sent away to eternal punishment (Matt 25:41–46). When a man asked Jesus to judge in the dividing of an inheritance he refused to do so and then spoke about greed as being a problem (Lk 9:25). In describing how people use money and material resources he used words that express self-centredness: arrogant, covetous, shrewd, greedy, lovers of money. He said people 'run after this', and they 'store it up'.

On the other hand Jesus spoke very positively about those who used their resources in their relationships with others. He tells the parable of the Good Samaritan who uses his money, oil, wine, bandages and donkey to come to the aid of the person who had been robbed and left for dead at the side of the road (Lk 10:30–36). He says that those who use their resources to feed the hungry and give accommodation and clothes to the needy are rewarded in heaven (Matt 25:31–40). He is very complimentary of the woman who uses her expensive perfume to anoint his feet (Lk 7:36–47). He encourages the rich to give to the poor, in this way he says they will store up treasure in heaven (Lk 12:33–34). He told people to give generously to others who were in need and not expect to get their goods back (Lk 6:30–38).

In the eyes of Jesus, material resources were not just to be used for selfish indulgence by those who possessed them. They were to be creatively utilised to bless, encourage and develop others less fortunate.

The Bible has a lot more to say about covetousness than it does about homosexuality.

One final insight from the life of Christ as he prays to the Father in John 17:10, Jesus says, 'All I have is yours all you have is mine'. Here we have a picture of joint ownership and co-operation. What belongs to the Father also belongs to the Son and what was the Son's was also the Father's. No selfishness, individualism or self-interest here. Autonomy does not feature in the relationships between the members of the Godhead. How can this verse be outworked in Christian relationships? What would happen if we put this statement over our marriages, families, congregations, home groups, leadership teams or our relationships with other local churches? It must mean that my resources, time, money, goals, dreams and spiritual gifts are to be shared with you and yours are to be shared with me. After all they all belong to God anyway. It would be interesting to see what would happen if local congregations committed themselves to each other in this way. This was the outworking of the relationship between Father and Son and is a reflection of the passion of Jesus for his people.

Starting point 4: The formation of the New Testament church

What was the greatest miracle in the early chapters of Acts? The fact that all the apostles spoke in tongues? The preaching of Peter on the day of Pentecost resulting in the conversion of 3,000 people? The healing of the cripple at the gate of the temple? The miraculous release of the apostles from prison? No doubt all of these were amazing events, but surely the greatest miracle must have been the way that the early Christians used their physical resources for each other. Only this touched the self-centredness of their human hearts. Healings, tongues, preaching, miraculous escapes, none of these touched it. These were gifts for God. What touched their self-centredness was the sharing of their resources – also a gift from God. This gift they gave back to God. Notice what they did:

- They shared things in common (Acts 2:44).
- They had close fellowship, shared belongings and distributed to those in need (Acts 2:45).
- They had meals together (Acts 2:46).
- They had one mind and heart, no one said their belongings were their own and they shared everything they had (Acts 4:32).
- No one in the group had need (Acts 4:34).
- Money was distributed to each according to need (Acts 4:35).

All the world lives in two tents – content and discontent

One of the words that expresses relationships between Christians in the New Testament is the Greek word for fellowship – *koinonia*. The root *koinon* is often linked to actual social and economic relationships between Christians. Consider these references:

- Acts 2:42,44 – they shared everything in common (*te koinonia*)
- Rom 12:13 – they shared hospitality (*koinonountes*)
- 1 Tim 6:18 – the rich are commanded to be generous (*koinonikous*)
- Rom 15:26 – the financial collection for Jerusalem Christians was an act of fellowship (*koinonian tina*)
- Gal 6:6 – those who were taught by a teacher were to share their good things with the teacher (*koinoneito*)
- 2 Cor 8:4, 9:13 – financial fellowship between the first-century Christians was seen in the collection for the Jerusalem Christians (*koinonia*).[1]

The miracle is this – the more we share the more we have.

Fellowship for the New Testament Christians went much further than just the social, the emotional or the spiritual dimensions, it clearly embraced the use of their material resources for each other.

There are clear links between the Old Testament socio-economic relationships and relationships between people in the New Testament church:

- In Acts 4:34 we read, 'There were no needy persons among them.' This is almost a direct quote from Deuteronomy 15:4, 'There will be no poor among you.'
- Paul illustrates giving by using the example of the gathering of the manna. As Israel travelled to their promised land God provided them food in the form of manna. It seems that some gathered extra for their families, for the young, the elderly or the sick who were unable to gather sufficient for themselves (Ex 16:16–18). Paul says that when it comes to material resources 'your plenty will supply what they need, so that in turn their plenty will supply what you need. Then there will be equality . . . (2 Cor 8:14–15). The statement about there being equality should not be interpreted in some socialist sense where everybody is required to have equal material resources. To interpret it this way would disregard both Old and New Testament indications that some people possess more material resources than others. It does not seem to be God's intention for everybody to have exactly the same amount of resources. 'There will be equality', probably means equal opportunity to contribute to the well-being of each other.
- There are strong statements made about greed in the New Testament. It is equated with idolatry (Eph 5:3–5, Col 3:5), a further link to Old Testament perspectives on material resources

This sort of language clearly indicates that relationships between people must embrace the use of material resources. This is what it means to be part of the redeemed community. Redemption that does not touch the use of our resources in our relationships with others has to be questioned as to whether or not it is true redemption.

> ***Christians in the West are driven by values and
> aspirations we have not checked and do not
> come from Scripture.***

Two further portions from the New Testament Church demand our attention. In 1 Timothy 6:17–19 Paul says to Timothy,

> Command those who are rich in this present world not to be arrogant nor to put their hope in wealth, which is so uncertain, but to put their hope in God, who richly provides us with everything for our enjoyment. Command them to do good, to be rich in good deeds, and to be generous and willing to share. In this way they will lay up treasure for themselves as a firm foundation for the coming age, so that they may take hold of the life that is truly life.

While in 2 Corinthians 9:11 we read, 'You will be made rich in every way so that you can be generous on every occasion, and through us your generosity will result in thanksgiving to God.' These two references linked with 1 John 3:16–18 (mentioned earlier in this chapter), clearly show the link between economic resources and relationships for Christians. In fact, in the New Testament giving is first and foremost to people, not buildings, not churches not missions, but Christians supplying financial aid to other Christians.

Starting point 5: The coming kingdom

There are only a few rather obscure indications of economic principles in the coming kingdom. A study of Luke 17:26–30, Isaiah 55:1 and Revelation 21:6 seem to indicate that there will be no buying or selling in heaven. Buying and selling is a human response, it is the way we protect our assets. God is not protective of his assets, he is extremely generous and wants his children to be like him. We experience God's generosity now and will do so for all eternity. God's response is giving and sharing. Generosity should be a family trait.

Relationships linked to resources

At each of the major initiation points we see material resources and human relationships intertwined. God intends that the resources of this planet be available to all. Poverty is not part of his initial intention nor his final kingdom, and the relationships between members of congregations must include the use of their physical resources for each other.

In God's eyes, our relationships together cannot be genuine or real if they do not involve the use of our material resources for each other. Such sharing requires us to be 'other-centred' and cuts right across the ethos of our materialistic society. The heart of our Christian faith is serving people rather than protecting self. Further, it is important that where Christian groups attempt this, the dignity and respect of all parties be maintained (see Appendices I and II).

Capitalism without the underpinning of the ten commandments and the stimulus of the Beatitudes soon degenerates into self-destructive greed.

We cannot and must not avoid the implications of this biblical evidence. It may be difficult for us as individualistic, materialistic, Western Christians to accept this as part of God's purposes for redeemed relationships. However if we are going to be true to those purposes, not only must we accept them but we must also embrace them as part of our relationships with other Christians.

Denis Peacock captures the truth of the matter about material possessions when he says,

> Humanity faces two poles: Selfish individualism and rigid collectivism. The first neglects human community, the second human freedom. Both place human beings at the centre of the world and reduce creation to a tool for humanity. The Biblical view is that of the freedom of the

individual to contribute to the needs of the community.

What is missing from modern capitalism is the obligation of giving to counterbalance the right of owning. E Stanley Jones makes this arresting statement, ' "Good news to the poor" means that every person has a right to as much of the material things as will make them mentally, spiritually and physically fit for the purposes of the Kingdom of God, the rest belongs to the needs of others.'[2] One could add a final phrase to this statement and say that 'the rest belongs to the needs of others to also make them mentally, spiritually and physically fit for the purposes of the kingdom of God'.

Let me summarise the main points that we have been seeking to make in this chapter. These are not the only economic principles outlined in Scripture,[3] but they embrace some of the more important ones that affect our relationships together.

a) Coming from the point of view of 'giving', our teaching on money and material possessions has been too limited. We need to see the topic of material resources from a broader view, that of Biblical Economics.

b) God owns everything, he has given this planet to humans to manage. This is the principle of stewardship.

c) Stewardship means that I cannot do whatever I like with my possessions. A steward's responsibility is to use what they have been given for the benefit of the owner.

d) However, stewards are not the same as slaves, they are given considerable freedom of expression.

e) Good stewards develop their character, abilities and gifts by faithful use of the resources that God has placed in their hands thus enhancing their effectiveness in God's kingdom

f) Exploitation is not God's intention for this planet, but productivity is.

g) God is concerned about the rich getting richer at the expense of the poor getting poorer. He set up mechanisms within Israel to prevent the downward slide into debt, poverty and bondage.

Progress – where half the world's population is over-worked and the other half unemployed.

h) God is totally opposed to those who profit from the misfortune of others.

i) When loans are made, the security of our money is of less importance than the well-being of the other person.

j) Money and material possessions hold an enormous power over our lives.

k) How we handle physical resources is an indication of our faithfulness to God.

l) Jesus spent a large amount of his time speaking about money and material possessions. Stewardship is the theme of many of his parables. Stewards are not owners.

m) Jesus is constantly negative about hoarded wealth. He sees it as an indication as to where our trust is.

n) God detests covetousness and greed.

o) Using our resources for others cuts at the heart of our self-centredness.

p) Fellowship (*koinonia*) in the New Testament church involved the sharing of their material resources.

q) The main form of giving in the New Testament was to others in need.

r) Those who have surplus resources are commanded to use their surplus for others.

s) The world's economic system is one of buying and selling, this protects our assets. God's response to us is giving and sharing.

t) God's intention is that everybody has sufficient material resources to get the job done he has for them.

u) Love is laying down my life for others. Laying down my life means using my resources for others.

Be careful that monetary success doesn't give you gold in your palm, silver on the tongue, brass in the face and iron in the heart.

We conclude this chapter with the following story that throws into sharp contrast the difference between the kingdom of God and the kingdom of this world in attitudes towards material resources.

When Alexander the Great came upon a village hidden in a remote part of Africa he discovered the people were peaceloving – they had never been involved in war. He was greeted warmly by all and taken as an honoured guest to the hut of the chief.

As the two leaders sat in conversation, two citizens entered the hut asking that the chief serve as a judge over their dispute.

'I bought a piece of land from this man,' the first began. 'While ploughing, I discovered a treasure which he refused to take. When I bought the land for a market price, I had no idea there would be anything of value buried on it.'

The second man was quick to speak.

'When I sold him the land, I gave up all rights to anything found on the property. The treasure clearly belongs to him.'

The chief summarised the arguments until both men indicated that he clearly understood the case. After some reflection, he spoke to the first man.

'You have a son, I believe?'

'Yes, sir'

'And you,' he said to the second, 'have a daughter!'

'Yes.'

'Let your son marry your daughter,' the chief concluded. 'Give the two of them the treasure as a wedding gift.' The two men looked at each other, nodded, and bowed to the chief before leaving.

Alexander expressed surprise over the verdict.

'Was my judgment unjust!' the chief asked.

'Oh, no,' Alexander said.

'What would you have done in your country?' the chief asked.

'In my country, either the men would have fought over the treasure to keep it for themselves or the government would have confiscated it.'

The chief was shocked. 'Does the rain fall in your land?'
'Yes.'
'Does the sun shine?'
'Yes.'
The chief thought for a moment.
'Are there animals that graze on the green grass?'
'Certainly,' Alexander replied, 'thousands of animals of different varieties.'
'Ah,' nodded the chief, 'it must be for the sake of the animals that the Lord causes the rain to fall and the sun to shine, for certainly the people in your land are not worthy of his great blessings.'

10

DOING IT BETTER

We were taking a break from one of those rather boring meetings that educationalists have to attend from time to time. In my role as a Science lecturer at Teacher's College, I was part of an oversighting committee for the development of new science courses in our area. One of the participants at this meeting was Peter,[1] the General Manager for Education in our region. As we sipped our cups of tea, Peter was reflecting on his many years of involvement in education.

'In my opinion,' he said, 'there is no more difficult a task in our modern society than being the principal of a high school.'

There were murmurs of agreement from around the group; several had been high school principals.

Peter continued.

'In my time as a principal I found it demanded so many skills. You had to be a visionary, a negotiator, a confidant, a manager, a financial expert and counsellor all rolled into one. You need the patience of Job and the wisdom of Solomon.'

'Throw in with that the hide of a rhinoceros,' interjected another member of the group.

'Then there are the long hours, the involvement with parents, the recalcitrant pupils and the need for increasing sensitivity in cultural matters,' Peter added.

More knowing nods from around the group.

As I sat there, I thought to myself – he has never pastored a congregation! At least in school situations you can motivate people with financial reimbursement and the prospect of promotion. No such enticements are afforded in a volunteer organisation such as a church. Here, there are very few if any privileges, no promotion, 24-hour on-call expectation, hostile spiritual opposition and the pay leaves much to be desired!

What structure holds a volunteer organisation like a congregation together? Well, there are two main ways that we can structure such an organisation – by regulations or by relationships. Most groups that are highly regulated will be light on relationships, whereas those that function from a relationship basis can afford to be lighter on regulations. Where there is trust, you do not need so many rules. Where there is trust, there is greater flexibility and therefore greater ability to modify and adjust to changing conditions and situations.

> *The test of courage comes when you are in the*
> *minority. The test of tolerance when you*
> *are in the majority.*

Most families and marriages work from the base of relationships and do not need many, if any, rules or regulations. It is when a marriage breaks down that the lawyers are called in to establish the rules and regulations. As far as we can tell, the Trinity is structured around relationships not regulations, around covenant not creed.

It is my belief that a congregation's main ethos should be that of relationship – light on rules but high on trust, commitment, love and honesty. Such an ethos offers the following significant possibilities:

a) It is an embracing, healing environment, where people feel wanted and supported. In many urban areas, people's lives are so mobile and hectic that there is no time for such relationships. A congregation should provide a healing environment.

b) It provides nutritive surroundings of trust, love and support. This is an ideal set of circumstances to optimise spiritual life and growth.

c) It encourages people to take the initiative and have a

go, rather than having to struggle through many procedures and rules in order to participate.

d) It enhances the ministry of the Holy Spirit. 'God commands a blessing when there is unity' (Ps 133). Unity cannot be created through regulation, it is something that comes out of relationship.

e) It permits changes and adjustments to occur more easily within the group. This is a crucial point in today's fast moving, rapidly changing society. Many churches have set up so many rules and regulations with committees for everything, that it takes them forever to bring changes.

f) It creates an appropriate environment for answered prayer. Jesus says agreement brings God's response (Matt 18:19). Agreement is unity in relationship.

Faith is the soul's intake. Love is the soul's outlet.

g) It provides a witness to two of the most crucial facts people outside of the Church need to know.
Firstly, who Jesus is – 'May they also be [one] in us so the world may believe that you have sent me' (Jn 17:21). Christian relationships should be such that they tell the world who Jesus is, that he is the Messiah and that he came from God.
Secondly, who we are – 'Love one another . . . By this all men will know that you are my disciples' (Jn 13:34–35). Christian relationships should be such that they tell the world who we are, that we are Christ's disciples.

h) It enhances evangelism. Most people come to faith in Christ through relationships with friends. To bring people into a relationship-based congregation where there is life, love and spontaneity encourages people in their quest to find Christ.

All too often Christian relationships can be very superficial. Mouth-to-mouth relationships are common, where we repeat nice pleasantries to each other as we pass in the foyer.

Mind-to-mind relationships go a bit further. We may actually get into discussion on some issue or problem or even the minister's sermon! Such superficial relationships are very safe, but quite sterile. God's intention is for heart-to-heart relationships among his people, where real and personal issues can be raised in an atmosphere of care, trust and honesty. How do we hear a person's heart? By listening intently, listening to them describe their feelings, listening with our eyes as well as our ears. One thing we can be sure of God is a good listener, he wants his children to be the same.

> *He drew a circle that shut me out; Heretic, rebel a*
> *thing to flout; But love and I had a mind to win;*
> *We drew a circle that took him in.*

It is easy to recognise a congregation where relationships have a high priority. People are more outgoing, they stay around and talk together after congregational services, they will approach newcomers and some will even come up and talk to the visiting preacher!

To enhance relationships within a congregation we need to take definite steps to structure for them. Below are some suggestions to this end.

For leadership

a) First and foremost, leadership needs to teach and pray into the area of relationships. In teaching and instruction leaders need to give the priority that the New Testament writers give to this topic. They need to help people see the passion of Jesus about this issue. Many congregations have teaching and instruction on almost everything else except this area.

b) Leadership teams need to model healthy relationships together. I have found that tense leadership situations are quickly discerned at a congregational level. People feel secure when leadership teams are secure.

c) A leader needs a team around him or her, this helps people to see that relationships are important. Teams in other areas of congregational life are also important. Teams need to be strengthened and relationships enhanced and deepened. Healthy relationships within a team mean that people's strengths can be released and weaknesses covered. This will be further discussed in the next chapter.

Watch each others' backs.

d) A congregational vision or statement of aims must stress the relationship component of congregational life. This needs to be a high priority.

For small groups

i) The congregation needs to be structured into small groups that meet in homes each week. It is here that real relationships develop.

ii) People need to get away together, over weekends or on retreats. We need to create many opportunities for social interactions, these enhance the development of relationships. It is important for small groups to get away for extended periods together.

iii) The opportunity for Communion in small (or cell) groups in homes brings an intimacy and deepening of relationships. I recognise that not all denominations would approve of this. However, my understanding is that Communion commenced in the upper room with Jesus and his disciples in an atmosphere of informality and friendship. It was continued in the homes of Christians during the first century.

iv) Social activities are important. Such things as lunches, picnics, outings, ten pin bowling and parties of various types, are good opportunities for relationships to be strengthened.

v) Work groups on people's properties or around the church facilities are opportunities for interaction and encourage friendships to develop.

vi) The use of homes for hospitality is recommended in

Scripture. This needs to be both spontaneous and from time to time organised.

'At the heart of personality is the need to feel a sense
of being lovable without having
to qualify for that experience.'
Maurice Wagner

vii) Prayer triplets, where three people covenant to pray with and for each other are also a good way to deepen relationships.

During congregational gatherings

a) Informal times of welcome during congregational services also have their place. Here people can mix and mingle.

b) Some congregations are incorporating a time for a cup of tea or coffee after, during or before the congregational service. This encourages people to spend a more relaxed time together.

c) Communion itself is a relationship-based activity. It indicates relationship with God and also relationship with each other. Communion often becomes a ceremony within the modern church. It is full of dignity and solemnity and a far cry from the first century, where it appears to have normally been held around meal tables probably within homes. Permitting small groups of people, or family groups to gather to share Communion within the congregational Communion service enhances the relationship dimension of this sacrament.

d) During the more formal congregational services there are a number of things that can be done which will enhance relationships at such a time –
   • prayer within small groups during the service,
   • small groups discussing a point raised during the sermon,
   • encouraging people's participation during the ser-

vice in the sharing of testimonies,

- questions from the floor or from the pulpit encouraging greater participation from the whole group. Not only do many of these things enhance the relationship dimension of a congregation but they are also better learning techniques.

e) The participation of the families during congregational services is important. Children will do things differently and may make mistakes but this creates a more informal atmosphere. Relationships flourish in informality rather than ceremony. Sometimes people object to informal services saying that they lack reverence. This may sometimes be true, but genuine reverence is an attitude of the heart rather than some contrived (or maybe even manipulated) formality.

f) Those involved in welcoming people have a vital role in encouraging relationships. They need to be warm outgoing people, able to make people feel relaxed and at home.

g) Bringing profiles on people or families during congregational services helps people to get to know others and strengthens relationships.

h) Encouraging friends and relatives to gather round those being prayed for in public is a supportive and helpful exercise. Such times could include commissioning for some special service, dedications of children, prior to baptisms or when praying for healing.

General areas

i) The design of the building and seating layouts will either hinder or contribute to the enhancement of relationships. Many churches have the seats fixed in position and facing the same way. This restricts relationships and if it can be addressed, it should be.

ii) Evangelism is best based on friendships. Encouraging a congregation towards deeper relationships should have added spin offs in the area of evangelism.

> *'Be tender with the young, compassionate with the*
> *aged, sympathetic with the striving and tolerant of*
> *the weak and strong. Because some day in your life*
> *you will have been all of these.'*
> **George Washington Calver**

iii) Encouraging congregational members to be involved
in local organisations is essential. Too many Christians
become so immersed in their congregation and
involved with their Christian friends that they lose
many of their non-church friends. Relationship links
need to be maintained.

iv) Financial support of each other enhances relationships
and, as was mentioned earlier, is an essential part of
biblical relationships.

v) Congregational sports teams are also great opportunities for the development of relationships.

No doubt there are many other things that can be done. One
thing is certain, if we are to enhance and strengthen relationships within congregational life, very little will occur unless
leadership teaches about them, plans for them and structures
for them.

11

TEAMS ARE IN

Everybody seems to be doing it! National sports teams bring in psychologists or go away together, not to train but to do it. Politicians from a particular political party spend weekends together, not discussing policies but doing it. Business executives take retreats, not to plan for greater productivity but to do it. Staff from companies go away, not for training but for activities in the outdoors to do it. Government departments encourage staff to do it. MBA courses in universities recommend it and the Japanese have been doing it for years.

The future organisational structures will not be paternalistic or rigid but fluid organic networks able to make decisions quickly.

Today it seems that team-making is in! Numerous groups in society spend many hours and a lot of money developing a corporate spirit. People are waking up to the fact that co-operation and teamwork within an organisation is a better way to go than competition. You get the best out of people when they relate together well. When their skills and abilities have been assessed and they are placed in positions within the organisation where they are best fitted. Square pegs go better in square holes than in round holes. In terms of productivity, leaders are finding that in harmonious teams 1 + 1 + 1 does not equal three but four or five or maybe even six.

Mind you, teams have been around for a very long time; actually they have been around for ever. God the Father, Son and Spirit were the first team. Teams are really as old as eternity. A team is a group of co-labourers who are co-existent, co-essential, co-equal and co-operatively working together to achieve a common purpose. Such also is the structure of the Trinity. Strange then, that it has taken us so long to catch on and strange also that it still seems so hard for people in teams to work really well together.

There is clear evidence of teams in Scripture. There were teams of musicians in the Old Testament. King David had his team of mighty men around him. Teamwork is seen in the building of the Jerusalem wall under Nehemiah. Jesus had a team of disciples and at one stage he sent them out in teams of two. Paul travelled in teams – maybe up to at least four-teen members in his team at one time. The whole idea of the Church being a body has at its core the idea of teamwork.

Teams are normally more effective than individuals. The effect of a team is much more than the sum of the individual parts. Leviticus tells us that 'five will put one hundred to flight [1:20] and one hundred will put ten thousand to flight [1:100]' (Lev 26:8). That is, one hundred people working together produce an effect per head that is five times more effective than five people working together. The effect of team work is multiplicative rather than additive.

Teams present great possibilities; support for each other, encouragement, shared load and less loneliness than when going it alone. However they also create many potential dif-ficulties; team members have to think of others, work in with people of different personalities, submit to others and work with other people's limitations and weaknesses. In my obser-vation the more creative the team the more potential diffi-culties that team will have. Maybe that is why music and worship teams often seem to have the most trouble in a con-gregation.

Over the past twenty-five years it has been interesting to notice how many churches have been opting for a team lead-ership model. The days when one key player calls all the shots seem to be over. Maybe the moral failure of some high profile ministries has contributed to this trend. There are very few successful one-person leaders in congregations –

superstars with many gifts – they are the exception. It is unwise and unhealthy to profile superstars and raise them up as models to others. Regularly I have cause to talk with leaders of congregations who have been suffering untold struggles because they themselves (or their congregation) have been comparing themselves with the superstar of another congregation. In such a situation all one can do is encourage them to bring a team around themselves and let others do what they cannot do.

There are also strengths and weaknesses in both the one-person and the team leadership models. These are outlined in Figure 4.

One of the problems with leadership of congregations is that their leaders often gravitate to this position because they have been successful in the secular world. There are clearly some advantages in this, such as experience gained in planning, communication and interpersonal relationships. However they may also bring with them secular models that may not necessarily be the right models for leadership in a church.

One thing is certain, teams depend on healthy relationships for successful functioning – trust, co-operation, loyalty, love, vulnerability, honesty, accountability, encouragement and many of the things that I have being talking about in the preceding chapters must occur if a team is to function effectively. At the leadership level of any congregation the healthy relationships of the leadership team will make or break the progress of the congregation. If leadership teams are formed just to get a job done, that is run the congregation, and do not spend time building their relationships, then cracks will probably appear when pressures come or controversy occurs. The time to build strong relationships is when things are going well. Ideally leadership teams need to come together around their common life rather than their common task. Their task should flow out of their lives together. It takes time to build a team and in our ever-increasingly pressured lives time is a commodity in short supply.

Single leader	Leadership team
Strengths: One individual's vision, drive, ability may be better utilised. Decision-making is easier. Actions may be achieved faster. Inspiration and initiative from a gifted individual can be very motivating for the followers.	**Strengths**: Shared load. Greater awareness of congregation's needs. People in congregation will have at least one person to relate to at leadership level. Wisdom is found in a multitude of counsellors. Prov 11:14, 15:22, 24:6 God's blessing is on those dwelling in unity. Ps 133:1–3
Weaknesses: Pride, loneliness and isolation can become problems. Possibility of being misguided. Lack of accountability. Greater chance of satanic attack, moral fall is disastrous. Heavy pressures on one person. Very few people have sufficient gifts and abilities to carry this off.	**Weaknesses:** Teams can become deadlocked. Veto rights may become a problem in decision making. Tensions may develop in relationships. Decision-making takes more time.

Figure 4: Single leader vs a team

Team building

There are many important principles that need to be followed if a strong team is to be built and these principles apply to any teams whether they be within or outside a congregation. Much has been written on this so I will mention just three principles which in my opinion are absolutely fundamental. They are bottom line issues for Christian teams.

i) Develop strong relationships

Many teams in Christian work fall into the trap of allowing all of their relationships together to revolve around the ministry that they are in. This creates a hot-house environment for these relationships and is very artificial. For the healthy development of relationships, members of a team need to also spend time together outside of their 'ministry' area. They need to socialise as well as spiritualise.

The devil's most useful weapon is apathy.

Here are some helpful team activities:

- Try to spend time away together, a weekend or at least a day.
- Socialise, share meals together, plan times of relaxation, have fun, go to a restaurant, see a film together, play sport together. The vigorousness of the sport may depend on the age of the team but mini-golf and ten-pin bowling are always good options.
- If spouses are not already involved, bring them in on as many occasions as possible.
- Plan social times together with spouses.
- Spontaneously drop in on each other.
- Take an interest in each others' family life, the needs of children; pray together for them.
- Discuss work and its related needs, joys and pressures.
- Use humour, talk together about earlier times in your lives, your childhood and teenage years.
- Discover how married couples met. Have an evening when you show old photographs to each other.

> ***Kindness is the oil that takes the friction out of life.***
> ***Better to be oil than grit.***

- Remember birthdays and other special occasions.
- Pray for each other's needs.
- Lay hands on each other and pray for each other's specific tasks within the team.
- Build up each other with encouragement and support.
- Share insights that God is giving from his Word.
- Pass around helpful books and good articles.
- Summarise a good article or book for other members of the team – keep each other on the cutting edge of issues and grow in your understanding of issues together.
- Share resources.
- Most of all develop attitudes of co-operation. When we are members of a leadership team we constantly need to ask ourselves this question, 'Is my first thought one of co-operation with my other team members?' If not, then what is my first thought?

ii) Understanding your own and others' gifts and abilities

Insecure team members can hold back the progress of a team. Insecurity can come from many sources. Such things as previous unpleasant experiences, lack of encouragement from family while a child and lack of understanding of one's gifting or place either within the team or within the organisation the team is leading.

In Romans 12:3 we read 'Do not think of yourself more highly than you ought, but rather think of yourself with sober judgment, in accordance with the measure of faith God has given you.' In chapter 6 we explored this verse more thoroughly and discovered that 'sober judgment' means that we know what our gifts and abilities are. Knowing who we are frees us to stand outside ourselves and more objectively assess the events that are going on around about us. We are not held captive by the events of life. It is of absolute importance that we spend time in teams discussing each others' gifts, abilities and roles within the team. If our relationships are strong enough we also need to be able to face our weaknesses within the support and love of a committed team. In this way we will be able to cover for each others' weaknesses and release each other into our strengths. Releasing others into their God-given gifts is intended to enhance my gifting. The gifts of the Spirit operate in a multiplicative manner each contributing to the enhancement of the others.

Recognising our weaknesses and strengths can reduce the potential for clashes or competition between team members. It can also create empathy between members. Recognising strengths and weaknesses brings accountability within the team and may prevent the 'shot in the foot' problems.[1] It is weaknesses that are the limiting factors in our ministry. We need to learn to work within the framework of our weaknesses and the weakness of other team members. This is largely a matter of accepting other team members just as they are and not trying to change them. Obviously we should be praying for change if this is needed, but it is not our job to 'sort out' other team members unless they give us the right to speak into their lives.

Never rise above servanthood.

It is specially important for full-time staff to form strong relationships with each other. This may help prevent burnout problems. Pastors need a supportive team around them where weaknesses can be admitted and accountability encouraged. I am glad that over the years I have had people around me who have called me to accountability. Sometimes I have been 'on the mat' at eldership. Several times I have put my full-time role on the line to assess whether or not it is time for a change.

Those who preach and teach should also look for and encourage feedback on the content and presentation of their material.

The true mark of a Christian community is not the absence of conflict but the presence of reconciliation.

iii) Be loyal to team members when with other people

It is important that members of the group you are leading see the leadership team relating well together; that they hear you acknowledging, honouring and joking with each other in private and public. Always defend team members in public, thrash out any disagreements or issues within the team behind closed doors. Never be critical of team members in front of other people. Trust is built on loyalty, loyalty means covering each other's back. There is nothing more divisive or damaging to a team than to have members talking critically about other team members within the group of people that the team is trying to lead. Never raise the team's dirty washing in public, maintain absolute confidentiality about matters discussed by the team. These points cannot be emphasised too much and they apply not only to teams but to any healthy relationships.

Teams need leaders

It has been said that when God wanted to get a job done he did not choose a committee, he chose a person. A committee is defined as a group of people who individually can do nothing but who as a group can meet and decide that nothing can be done. We never see monuments erected to committees, they are normally erected in recognition of individuals.

When we come to discuss the topic of leadership in teams there are two central issues. For some groups there is a reluctance to recognise leadership while for others the issue is not whether or not there should be leadership, the issue is what sort of leadership will be exhibited. My own background (Open Brethren) has struggled with the first issue. Here eldership teams have often been indecisive because of lack of leadership. Such people have inevitably become frustrated within the congregational structure and sought opportunities for expression of the gifting outside of the congregation.

> *Many people have a problem with leadership some*
> *want more and some want less.*

Many of the best people from my own denomination have finished up in para-church organisations because the denomination as a whole has failed to recognise gifted leaders. Others have left the denomination entirely and found fulfilment within other groups where leadership is recognised and encouraged.

However other denominations, where leadership is accepted and encouraged, also have struggles in the area of leadership. Here the problem is often the way that the leader operates. Unfortunately it is possible to find the wrong people in leadership with the right motivation or the right people operating in the wrong ways.

Evidences of leadership
i) Biblical evidences
There is an indication of leadership in the Godhead. The Father is always seen as the 'source' of initiative. The Father sent the Son. Jesus prayed that the Father would send the Spirit. While on earth Christ always sought the will of the Father. God exalted Christ and placed him in the highest place.

We see clear evidences of leadership in the Old Testament. God chose leaders to lead his people. People such as Abraham, Joseph, Moses, Joshua, Deborah, Miriam, David, Ezra and Nehemiah spring to mind. Kings and prophets also had a role here. Speaking of David, Isaiah 55:4 says 'Behold, I have given him for a witness to the people, a leader and commander to the people.' We may say that this is Old Testament, times were different then. In the New Testament we have the example of Christ and the ministry of the Holy Spirit; leadership is no longer needed. However it is difficult to see how the life, death and resurrection of Christ and the giving of the Holy Spirit, has altered the need for God's people to recognise leadership.

Leadership is seen in the New Testament church. At the

day of Pentecost, Peter clearly took the lead. Maybe he had had a leadership role among the disciples when Jesus was here and this naturally continued after Christ's ascension. An example of this would be his 'I'm going fishing' statement after the death of Jesus at which several other disciples said they would also come. Peter's leadership role is also seen in that he was the apostle to the Jews. Further, Paul obviously led an apostolic team as he took his missionary journeys, while James seems to have had a leadership role in Jerusalem.

The leader's task is to create an environment that enables others to flourish.

Leadership gifts are given to the Church. There are at least three places in Scripture that indicate leadership is primarily a gifting. In 1 Corinthians 12:28 we read that 'God has appointed . . . gifts of administration' (Greek *kubernesis*). The Greek word *kubernesis* means to guide, govern, steer. It is the idea of the person who has his or her hand on the tiller. In Ephesians 4:11 we read, 'He gave some apostles . . . ' A study of other portions of the New Testament indicates that the gift of apostleship had leadership functions associated with it.[2] While in Romans 12:8 Paul writes, 'If [a man's gift is leadership] (Greek *proistemi*, to stand before, lead, rule) let him govern diligently.'

It is noteworthy that leadership gifts appear in each of the three main lists of gifts in the New Testament. As with other gifts, leadership has to be developed, matured, regulated and honed. To reject the gift of leadership is to reject the sovereignty of God in providing the gift and hence to frustrate the purposes of God for us.

One of the problems congregations can get themselves into is in the appointment of a shepherd or pastor. Often someone with pastoral gifting is not necessarily a leader and when such a person tries to lead, all sorts of confusion and insecurities within a congregation develop. He or she is placed in a very difficult situation – if employed by the group then inevitably that person will know much more about what is going on within the congregation living it, eating it and sleeping it. This will increase the pressure on such a pastoral person to try to get in and sort things out or lead, maybe with disastrous results. I have come to the conclusion that at least one of the employed staff within a congregation must have leadership gifting. However if this is so, then further safe-guards need to be in place to prevent the misuses of 'power'. We come to this later.

> *'True leaders are marked by loyalty, for they seek*
> *another's cause; by fidelity, for they tell another's*
> *truth; by humility, for they accept another's results;*
> *by constancy, for they wait for another's time;*
> *and by expectancy, for they dream of another's glory.'*
> *Leighton Ford*

ii) Other evidences of leadership
There have been many notable Christian leaders down through history. The history of the Church is largely the history of leaders who have created change. Luther, Wesley, Whitfield, Moody, General Booth, Livingstone and Carey were all leaders anointed and gifted by God at particular times to carry out special ministries. Women such as Catherine Booth and Madame Guyon also feature among the leaders whom God has raised up. Then there are the more recent leaders that have established major ministries around the world: Loren Cunningham, Bill Bright, Billy Graham, Jackie Pullinger. Most, if not all growing churches today are associated with a strong recognised leader. Many of these leaders gather a team around them and the best of them work in consultation with the congregation and make them-selves accountable to others.

Those groups who do not recognise leadership gifts at the governmental level for the whole congregation, appear inconsistent when they gladly appoint recognised leaders in such activities as Sunday School, youth ministry, small groups and music.

Then there are the evidences of leadership in the 'secular' world; managing directors in businesses, principals of schools, heads of government departments, presidents, prime ministers, the armed forces, the police, captains of planes and ships all witness to the same thing – people need leadership. Leadership is a quality found to a greater degree in certain people.

> *Leadership is the art of getting others to do some-*
> *thing that you want done because they want to do it.*

Recognition, release and regulation of leadership

What are the qualities of a God-gifted leader? How are they recognised? Who recognises them? Who appoints them?

The following would seem to be a few of the qualities of Christian leadership. A person –
- whom people follow
- who has high moral integrity
- who can make decisions
- who sees a way ahead through difficult situations
- who plans for the future
- who is able to release and encourage others in their ministry
- who can work with a team
- who can accept and respond to correction (essential for all giftings!) and criticism.
- who is spiritually sensitive
- who has time to do the job
- who is willing to be accountable

We bring blessing to ourselves (and our congregations) and enhance our own gifting when we recognise and release this gift among us. Leadership gifts need to be released within the context of a team of people committed to relationships where positive attitudes such as trust, respect, humility, honesty, transparency and accountability underpin everything that is done. Leaders, most of all, need to address negative attitudes such as hurt, pride, self-confidence, independence and ego in their own lives.

One of the difficulties with leadership is that it is a thing of 'spirit' and when we try to regulate it too much we lose something of the dimension of what God intends. Where relationships are a high priority, regulations about leadership do not need to play such a great part.

Only trust servant leaders

Leadership is a gifting and a role – it has nothing to do with domination or power. The best leadership, whether it be within the Christian Church or any other organisation, is servant leadership. Jesus was the supreme leader and he said his prime motivation was to serve. He specifically forbids his followers to 'lord it' over others (Matt 20:25–28). To be great in the kingdom of God a person becomes a servant, just as Jesus came not to be served but to serve.

- Servant leaders lay down their lives for others.
- Servant leaders are in leadership to make it possible for the desires, needs and aspirations of others to be fulfilled, not to fulfil their own desires, needs and aspirations.
- Servant leaders create an environment where others can flourish and reach their potential.
- Servant leaders do not hold onto authority, but can let it go with ease.
- Servant leaders rejoice when others excel.
- Servant leaders say, 'Stand on my shoulders, go beyond where I have led you.'
- Servant leaders are not interested in status or the trappings of authority.
- Servant leaders see a bigger picture than just their own involvement and can stand back letting others take over in order for that picture to be achieved.
- Servant leaders are constantly learning, they look for and take advice from others.
- Servant leaders know who they are in God, they have a sound assessment of their abilities.
- Servant leaders make themselves accountable and vulnerable.
- Servant leaders know how to listen to others and hear others' hearts.

- Servant leaders have learned how to grow through their own failures. They know the truth of the statement, 'Success in moving from one failure to the next without losing enthusiasm.'[3]
- Servant leaders are genuinely humble people.

> *'The essential responsibility of a leader is to define reality. The last is to say thank you.*
> *In between the leader is a servant.'*
> **Max Dupree**

Moses is a good example of a servant leader. He did not grasp after power. He was reluctant to take on the role of leader of the people of Israel when God called him. He took advice from his father-in-law who saw that Moses was burdened down with judging the people. He delegated authority to others and got them to judge the people. By-and-large he was very patient with the people of Israel, even though they complained regularly. He sought God's direction in his leadership of them. He overcame the 'pride test' – when God offered to make a great nation of him, he refused. He was committed to the bigger picture – that of bringing God's people into their land, and he urged God to destroy him rather than Israel, when Israel proved to be wayward.

One thing is certain, there are few things more rewarding than being part of a team of people who love the Lord, who are committed to establishing his kingdom and are also committed to each in strong bonds of love, support and encouragement. On the other hand there are few places more difficult to be in than a team of people who claim to be seeking to serve God but where there is mistrust, suspicion, rivalry and infighting.[4]

We will conclude this chapter with a parable that highlights both the possibilities and the potential problems facing teams.

A flock of quail lived near a marsh and they would fly to the nearby fields every day to feed. The only problem was that there was a Bird Hunter who lived nearby, and of late he had snared many quail in his net to take them to a nearby market to be sold. The reason he had grown so successful in catching them was that he had learned to imitate perfectly the call of the Leader. The Bird Hunter gave the call, and the quail, thinking it was the Leader, flew to his area where he tossed his net over them and captured them.

One day the Leader called all the quail together for a conference. He said, We are becoming decimated! Soon there will be none of us left. The Bird Hunter is catching us all, but I have found out how he does it. He learned my call and deceives you, but I have a plan. The next time you hear what you think is my call and fly to the area and the Bird Hunter throws his net on top of you, here is what you are to do: all together you stick your heads through the openings in the net, and in one motion fly up with the net and land on the thorn bush. The net will stick there, you extricate yourselves, and the Bird Hunter will have to spend all day freeing his net.'

And this is what they did. The Bird Hunter came, gave the imitation call, and the quail came. When the net was thrown over them, as one body they stuck their heads through the openings, and flew away to the thorn bush. They left a frustrated Hunter trying all day to get his net loose. This went on for some time until the Hunter's spouse bitterly complained that her husband was bringing home no quail to sell at the market. They were becoming poor. The Bird Hunter listened to his wife, told her of the actions of the quail, and with his hand on his chin, added, 'Be patient, dear wife. Just wait till they quarrel. Then we shall catch them again.'

> *One hundred pianos tuned to the same tuning fork*
> *are automatically in tune with each other. They are*
> *in harmony not because they are tuned to each other*
> *but because they bow to an external standard.*

Well, it so happened that one day when the Bird Hunter made his call, all the quail rose up and flew to the area where he was. As they were landing, one quail accidentally brushed against another.

'Will you watch where you're going, you clumsy ox,' cried

the one quail. The other said hastily,

'Oh, I'm sorry. I really am. I didn't mean to do it. It was an accident.'

'An accident, was it?' cried the first quail. 'If you watched where you're going instead of peering all about, you wouldn't be so clumsy.'

'Well,' said the second quail, 'I don't know why you take that attitude. I said I was sorry, and if you can't accept that. . . .' And they got to quarrelling. Soon the others, perceiving the argument, gathered around and took sides, one for the first quail and the other for the second.

Meanwhile, the Bird Hunter had his net ready and threw it over the birds. They began to cry to one another, 'Come, let us stop arguing and hurry or else we'll be caught. Let's fly over that way!'

The other quail responded, 'No, we're always flying over that way. We're always doing what you people want. Come, let us fly this way!' And while they were arguing which way to go, the Bird Hunter, with a smile on his face, gathered them up in the net, brought them to market, and that day made a fine penny.

THE AWESOME POWER OF WORDS.

There is a story told of a man who went to a rabbi with a question.

'Rabbi,' he said, 'I understand why God commands us not to kill or steal, but I do not understand why we should not tell lies against our neighbour.'

The rabbi replied, 'There is an answer and I will give it to you, but first I want you to get some feathers and place one on the doorstep of each house in the village. When you have done this come back to me and I will give you the answer.'

The man did as he was told and returned to the rabbi.

'Now Rabbi, what is the answer to my question?'

'Ah,' said the rabbi, 'There is one more thing I want you to do before I give you the answer. Go back and pick up all the feathers.'

'I cannot do that,' protested the man, 'It would be impossible as all the feathers will have been blown away by the wind.'

'That's what it's like with lies we tell against our neighbours,' said the rabbi, 'They are like feathers, we can never retrieve them.'

I've never been hurt by anything I didn't say.

We could not finish discussing this topic of relationships without briefly looking at how our words affect our relationships.

Speech must be our most powerful faculty. Consider the

effect of words
- the lilt and rhyme of poetry
- the sweet nothings between lovers
- the forceful intensity of the sport's coach, urging on his charges
- the rising crescendo of an argument between two protagonists
- the inflaming power of Hitler's oratory
- the mesmerising ability of the words of the advertising industry
- the smooth talk of politicians as they extricate themselves from difficult positions
- the persuasive words of the salesperson
- the graffiti on the wall
- the solemnity as the judge passes his sentence
- the urgency of a mother looking for her child

***It is difficult to say the right thing in the right place,
but harder to leave unsaid the wrong thing
at the provoking moment.***

Speech is our most powerful faculty, it gives out, whereas most of our other faculties take in. When we speak we are directing an activity towards others. True, some people speak to themselves, but this is not what speech is for. We primarily use words for others. Words, more than anything else, shape and form our relationships. From the earliest years a baby is subject to words of love and encouragement and very quickly learns to distinguish its mother's voice from the many others that coo over it. Children learn to respond to the different tones in their parent's words; anger, support, encouragement, commands, information. Grandparents, friends, sports coaches and school teachers and many other human relationships depend on words for their existence. God has spoken to humanity and still speaks today. We speak and sing words to God. Countless words are spoken in churches around the world. The great majority of gifts of the Spirit are word gifts. Words either enhance or destroy relationships and without them meaningful relationships would not exist.

Refuse to speak until you are ready to speak.

We speak hundreds of words a day in all manner of situations and yet we never speak a neutral word. There is no middle position with words, all words have some significance. What we say is either helpful or unhelpful, creative or destructive, positive or negative. Words may explain, soothe, inspire, create faith or they may destroy, incite, inflame or create doubt. Even idle words are either harmful or helpful. The two lists in Figure 5 clearly show how much difference spoken words can make in situations.

Think of many of the relationship situations in Scripture where words were either helpful or unhelpful.

- The words of agreement between Abraham and Lot as they separated (Gen 13).
- The words of deceit of Rebekah and Jacob as they conspired against Esau and Isaac (Gen 27).
- The cunning words of Delilah to Samson as she seeks to discover where his strength lies (Jdg 16).
- The words of compassion from Joseph as he finally tells his brothers who he is (Gen 45).
- The words of love between Naomi and her daughters-in-law as she bids farewell to Moab to return to Israel (Ruth 1).
- The words of friendship between David and Jonathan (1 Sam 20:42).
- The words of confrontation from Nathan to David after his sin with Bathsheba (2 Sam 12).
- The words of treachery from Absalom towards his father David (2 Sam 15).
- The threatening words from Jezebel to Elijah that caused him to flee for his life (1 Kgs 19:2).
- The words of encouragement and inspiration that caused the people of Israel to rebuild the wall under Nehemiah's leadership.
- The empty words of Job's friends as they seek to explain his misfortunes.

CREATIVE WORDS	DESTRUCTIVE WORDS
Helpful **Positive** **Good**	**Unhelpful** **Negative** **Bad**
Encouragement Advice Truth Instruction, teaching Information Praises Word gifts of Holy Spirit Support Correction, reproof, rebuke Honour Wisdom Rejoicing	Discouragement Rumour Lies Gossip Flattery Curses Blasphemy Jeers, taunts Condemnation Sarcasm Foolishness Grumbling

Figure 5 – Words are either positive or negative

Such examples show us what a huge difference spoken words can make in relationships between people, never neutral, either helpful or unhelpful, creative or destructive.

This lack of neutrality in words is further described in Scripture. We are commanded to say what is helpful, not harmful. 'Do not let any unwholesome talk come out of your mouths, but only what is helpful for building others up according to their needs, that it may benefit those who listen' (Eph 4:29). We are told that by our words we will either be acquitted or condemned and that we will be asked to give an account for every word spoken (Matt 12:36–37). We read that 'death and life are in the power of the tongue' (Prov 18:21). James further tells us that the tongue is capable of blessing and cursing (Jas 3:9). Unwholesome or helpful, acquitted or condemned, blessing or cursing – all stark comparisons illustrating the extremes to which words can be put.

A sharp tongue is no indication of a keen mind.

Destructive words, that spoil and break relationships, grieve the Holy Spirit (Eph 4:29–31). On the other hand the filling of the Holy Spirit produces creative words. 'Be filled with the Spirit. Speak to one another with psalms, hymns and spiritual songs. Sing and make music in your heart to the Lord, always giving thanks to God the Father for everything' (Eph 5:18–20).

Because words have this intrinsic power, we must take responsibility for everything we say (or write). We are not to be like particular personalities of whom it is said, 'they speak first and think later'!

Not only are the actual words spoken important but the way we speak them is also highly significant. The tone, the volume, the facial expressions and the body language all add power to the spoken word.

Think of the words of Jesus – always creative, never destructive. There was the ruler who said to Jesus, 'Speak the word and my servant will be healed.' The words Jesus spoke that rebuked the storm. The commands that ordered the spiritual authorities out from the demonised. The words of life and peace that he spoke to the crowds. The testimony of the soldier, 'Nobody ever spoke like this man.' Even the sharp words to the hypocritical religious leaders were intended to be corrective to his listeners.

Unfortunately congregations of Christians can all too often become hot-houses full of words. Here are some suggestions about the use of words in congregational relationships, these will prevent many misunderstandings.

a) We will never have an accurate account on an event second-hand, much less third, fourth, fifth or sixth hand. We must be careful that we do not jump to conclusions too quickly. Many relationships have been spoiled because statements, several steps removed from their source, have been taken at face value.

b) We need to be careful of statements made during emotion, either from others towards ourselves or from our-

selves. We often live to regret what was said in the heat
of the moment.

> **'The right word may be effective, but no word was
> ever as effective as a rightly timed pause.'**
> **Mark Twain**

c) There are always two sides to the same story. Do not
judge on one side only. I have lost count of the number
of times I have got all steamed up when I have discovered something about a situation only to hear a totally
different version from the other person. Consider the
following situation where there is one object but two
totally different viewpoints.

Viewpoint 1: I saw a picture of the Queen of
England. On her head was a small crown and she was
wearing a loose-fitting dress.

Viewpoint 2: It was a beautiful clear day off the
coast. Against the background of a mountain, with the
wind blowing from the West, I see a sailing ship.

What is this describing? It's describing the two sides
of New Zealands fifty cent coin. Remember there are
always two sides to every story and these sides may be
very different.

If we learn something unpleasant about someone, does it
have to be passed on, even if true?

A preacher once reminded an audience that God had given
us two ears and one mouth. We should listen twice as much
as we talk, or in the words of James 1:26, 'We should keep a
tight rein on our tongue.'

> ***It has been said that many people have the gift of the
> gab but do not know how to wrap it up.***

The writer of the book of Proverbs had many things to say
about words. Consider these wise words about words.[1] It
may be worthwhile placing them on a sheet and attaching
them in some place where they can be read. We have them
on a lavatory door at eye level when sitting!

9:7-8: If you rebuke a mocker, you will only get a smart retort; yes, they will snarl at you . . . A wise person, when rebuked, will love you all the more.

10:14: A wise person holds their tongue. Only a fool blurts out everything they know.

10:19-20: Don't talk so much. You keep putting your foot in your mouth. Be sensible and turn off the flow! When a good person speaks, they are worth listening to, but the words of fools are a dime a dozen.

11:13: A gossip goes round spreading rumours, while a trustworthy person tries to quiet them.

12:13-15: Lies will get a person into trouble, honesty is its own defence. Telling the truth gives a person great satisfaction. A fool thinks he needs no advice, but a wise person listens to others.

12:18: Some people like to make cutting remarks, but the words of the wise soothe and heal.

12:25-26: Anxious hearts are very heavy but a word of encouragement does wonders! A good person asks advice from friends.

13:1: A wise youth accepts his father's rebuke.

13:3: Self-control means controlling the tongue! A quick retort can ruin everything.

13:10: Pride leads to arguments; be humble, take advice and become wise.

13:18: If you refuse criticism you will end in poverty and disgrace; if you accept criticism you are on the road to fame.

15:1: A soft answer turns away wrath, but harsh words cause quarrels.

**It took Sir William Ramsay 16 years to discover
helium; the Curies 30 years to find radium;
but in less than five minutes some can produce tedium.**

15:4: Gentle words cause life and health; griping brings discouragement.

15:23: Everyone enjoys giving good advice, and how wonderful it is to be able to say the right thing at the right time!

15:31–32: If you profit from constructive criticism you will be elected to the wise person's hall of fame. But to reject criticism is to harm yourself and your own best interests.

16:24: Kind words are like honey – enjoyable and healthful.

16:27–28: Idle hands are the devil's workshop; idle lips are his mouthpiece. Gossip separates the best of friends.

18:8: What dainty morsels rumours are. They are eaten with great relish!

18:20–21: Ability to give wise advice satisfies like a good meal! Those who love to talk will suffer the consequences. People have died for saying the wrong thing!

19:20: Get all the advice you can and be wise the rest of your life.

23:12: Don't refuse to accept criticism; get all the help you can.

26:20: Fire goes out for lack of fuel, and tensions disappear when gossip stops.

26:22: Gossip is a dainty morsel eaten with great relish.

***Speak when you are angry and you will make the
best speech you will ever regret.***

28:13: A person who refuses to admit their mistakes can
never be successful. But if they confess and forsake
them, they get another chance.

28:23: In the end, people appreciate frankness more than
flattery.

29:1: The person who is often reproved but refuses to
accept criticism will suddenly be broken and never
have another chance.

How awesome is the power of words. They can:
- create or destroy relationships,
- build up or break down relationships,
- encourage or discourage relationships,
- praise or curse relationships,
- make or break relationships

the choice is ours.

A Parable for our Time

It was a hot afternoon as Jacob, the Samaritan olive-trader, wound his way carefully along the road to Jerusalem. He had been this way many times before but he was always cautious because of the bandits that frequently hounded passing travellers. His donkey trudged along flicking the flies off its flanks, occasionally stumbling as its foot struck a loose stone on the road. A Jewish priest hurried in the opposite direction, with no acknowledgment of Jacob's presence. That didn't surprise Jacob; Jews had not the slightest respect for Samaritans – but then the feeling was mutual.

'Sanctimonious old fool,' thought Jacob as the priest moved on down the road. Then his attention returned to the prospect of trade later that day. Business had been difficult recently and Roman taxes had sharply increased a month ago. He was worried about his credit rating and his wife was agitating for him to purchase a new home in Samaria.

Every human need is an opportunity for the love of God to be expressed in sacrificial action.

As he came round a corner his eye caught sight of what appeared to be a bundle of clothes at the side of the road some fifty metres ahead. Jacob stiffened. Was this a trap, laid by bandits to divert an unsuspecting traveller's attention? He drew closer and to his surprise realised it was a man – a Jew. He had been badly beaten, was unconscious and barely alive. Blood stained the side of the road, flies settled on the open

wounds; the man groaned. Jacob thought quickly. What
should he do? What could he do? Obviously the priest
would have seen the man. Why hadn't he done something
for his Jewish compatriot? Jacob stopped and dismounted
his donkey to take a cautious, closer look. The man groaned,
his eyes briefly opened and then closed again as he lapsed
back into unconsciousness. Jacob suddenly felt a wave of
compassion come over him. The man looked to be in his
early twenties, about the age of his eldest son. Quickly Jacob
reached for his water bottle and began to bathe his most serious wounds. He bandaged them up to prevent further loss of
blood and forced a little wine into the man's mouth. Then,
with the ease of someone accustomed to hoisting heavy bags
of olives, he laid him across his donkey, slapped his donkey
and set off at a trot toward Jerusalem.

> *Do only what is required of you and remain a slave.*
> *Do more than is required and become free.*

He wondered what he should do with his new charge. He
had no idea who the man was or where he lived. That information would have to wait until he regained consciousness.
Jacob remembered that there was a small inn on the outskirts
of Jerusalem. He had stayed there one evening about a year
ago. Maybe he could find accommodation for them there for
the night. All thought of trading that day was now gone.
Arriving at the inn he was pleased to find that there was a
room available. He carried the man in and laid him gently on
the bed. That evening Jacob looked after him, washed his
wounds, and when he regained consciousness, gave him
something to eat.

Next morning he paid the innkeeper two silver coins and
asked him to look after the man until he was well enough to
continue on his way. Before he left, Jacob promised to return
within the week and reimburse the innkeeper for any further
expenses that may have been incurred by the man's stay.

This parable was told by Jesus (in a slightly different way)
when asked by a legal expert to define a neighbour. It is
found in Luke 10:25–37. In the parable Jesus not only

explained who a neighbour was but also explained what it means to love.

This is a significant parable for our day and illustrates many of the points made about relationships in the previous chapters of this book. Let us use the story to illustrate several points.

My neighbour may be a person of a different culture

Although we do not know for sure that the man lying by the roadside was a Jew, it seems most likely that this was the case. Why would Jesus specify that the other man was a Samaritan? There was great animosity between Jews and Samaritans and that Samaritan had no reason whatsoever to help the man lying by the roadside.

It's no chore to love the whole world,
my problem is loving my neighbour next door.

Establishing relationships with people of different cultures from ourselves is not easy. They think differently, react differently, speak differently. We are embarrassed when we make cultural blunders. I can remember being dismayed when I discovered that I had been very culturally insensitive by passing food to people in India using my left hand. I am left-handed – I'll let you discover why it was culturally insensitive! It is often hard work establishing relationships in other cultures. We are much more comfortable with those who are like ourselves.

According to this parable my neighbour may be of a different culture to myself.

My neighbour may also be in my congregation or my home group.

My neighbour may be a person of different economic status

As far as that Samaritan was concerned the man by the side of the road was the poorest of the poor; stripped, beaten, dusty, lying by the road and covered with flies – you can't get much poorer than that. It is sometimes difficult for us to establish relationships with people of very different economic status, especially a lower one. It is of greatest importance that we seek to take steps to bridge this gulf.

Some years ago I was invited to preach in a congregation in Auckland. As I came up the road towards the church I was aware that I was in a lower socio-economic area. The homes had been built by the Government around the 1960s; there were no fences, concrete driveways that had broken up, not many trees, old cars outside, scruffy little children playing in the street. As I approached the church I was suddenly aware of a difference. The cars outside were of modern vintage and stepping out of them were very well-dressed parents and children.

After the service I asked one of the leaders about the congregation and discovered that all of those attending lived outside the area and travelled to the church from affluent areas. Their intention was to evangelise the area in which the church was placed.

As I drove back along the street that day I wondered how many local people would have ever come into that church and if they did, whether they would feel comfortable there. I was not at all surprised two years later, when I heard that the church had closed its doors deciding that the area was 'too tough'.

According to this parable my neighbour may be of different economic status to myself.

My neighbour may also be in my congregation or my home group.

My neighbour may be a person of different physical condition

The man lying in the gutter would not have been the coolest person on the face of the earth. To have been seen with him would not gain you many credits in the high society columns of the daily newspapers.

Do we find it easy to relate to those of a different physical condition to ourselves? The handicapped, the sick, the unlovely, those with embarrassing mannerisms or characteristics like bad body odour.

> *Jesus washing the disciples' feet is a statement about servanthood, youth and women.*
> *Only girl slaves washed people's feet*

Some years ago a young lady in our congregation was working among young people at risk. She would often visit the homes of these young people to discuss matters with the children's parents. One Saturday she was visiting a home. It's always difficult to visit on Saturday – come too early and people are still in bed, come too late and they've gone out for the day. As she knocked on the door she wondered if there was anybody at home. She knocked again and from deep within the house she heard a muffled cry of, 'I'm coming.' Suddenly the door was flung open and there stood the girl's six-foot father clothed in nothing but his underpants. The youth leader was only five feet tall and the first thing that she saw was not the underpants, but the fleas on his hairy chest! She had to go into that home, sit in the armchair in the lounge and talk to that parent about his daughter.

According to this parable my neighbour may be of different physical condition to myself.

My neighbour may also be in my congregation or my home group.

> *'Preach the gospel at all time and if necessary, use words.'*
> **Francis of Assisi**

Love is using my time for others

The details that Jesus puts in this parable are significant. We read that the Samaritan 'went to him' (v 34). He went out of his way and interrupted his schedule to spend time with this man. The Samaritan stayed overnight with him. How many hours interruption would that have been? Let's assume that he found the man at 3.00 pm and left him next morning at 9.00 am. That would be eighteen hours spent with this stranger, who could also potentially have been an enemy. Relationships take time, and time is the only commodity that we all have the same amount of, twenty-four hours a day, one hundred and sixty-eight hours a week. Time is the most precious commodity that anyone can possess – in fact it is so valuable that it is rationed, we get only one moment at a time. As was explained earlier in chapter 9, I lay down my life when I use my time for others. It is always interesting to see how some people can get much more out of their time than others.

Over the years we have had people in our congregation who have been involved in the resettlement of refugees; this takes time, lots of it – time to go with them to the bank, the school, to show them the ropes of our culture, to help them improve their English. It is very costly in terms of our own schedules.

According to this parable, love may mean using my time for others.

It may also mean using it for those in my congregation or my home group.

Love is using my possessions and money for others

This Samaritan used his donkey, his oil, his wine, his bandages and his money – two silver coins, the equivalent in those times of two days' wages. In chapter 9 I sought to show how central this concept of using our resources for others is in God's understanding of relationships. In this parable, told by Jesus, we see it again. A recent poll in the USA showed that Christians who earn between $50,000 and $75,000 a year give only 1.5 per cent to charity, religious or otherwise, while they spend 12 per cent on their leisure pursuits. What a sad evidence of our self-centredness and our reluctance to use our resources for others.

> *'That which you cannot give, you do not possess.*
> *It possesses you.'*
> *Ivern Ball*

According to this parable, love may mean using my possessions and money for others.

It may also mean using them for those in my congregation or my home group.

Love is using my abilities for others

We all have three types of ability. Natural talents, which we are born with. Acquired skills, which we develop in life, and spiritual gifts that God gives to us to use in his service. This Samaritan used these three abilities to help the man on the road side that day. He seems to have had a strong healthy body – a natural talent – he was able to hoist the man onto his donkey. He had some acquired skills – he bandaged up the man's wounds. He had a spiritual gift – the gift of mercy – he had compassion on the man.

Sometimes we think that we haven't got very much to give. Sometimes we get the impression that spiritual gifts are where it is really at. Given to him, God can employ any ability that we have for the blessing of others and the extension of his kingdom.

In the Old Testament, David used his acquired skill (a sling) to lead God's people to a great victory over their enemies, while on another occasion he used his natural talents (music) to soothe a demonic king. Did David have a spiritual gift? Well, technically no – these were given after Christ ascended to heaven. However, it seems reasonable to believe that David had a spiritual gift, the gift of leadership. This was not an ability that he would have had much cause to develop, unless you count leading sheep! He was the youngest son in a family and was not even in the line up that Jesse ordered when Samuel was sent by God to Jesse's family to anoint the next king of Israel. Scripture records that after Samuel anointed David to be the next king of Israel, the Spirit of the Lord came upon him from that day on. Within a few chapters, empowered by the Spirit, he is striding out to fight Goliath and lead Israel to a famous victory.

What a huge variety of resources God has given us to minister to others with whom we have relationships. Everybody has got something to use for others.

According to this parable love may mean using my abilities for others.

It may also mean using them for those in my congregation or my home group.

We all have only three commodities in this life – time, possessions and abilities. Nothing else with which to serve God and others. Love is using these three commodities for others.

Ultimately Christian faith is a very simple matter. Our parable emphasises this. It is a two-way relationship – a vertical or personal relationship with God – we are to 'love the Lord our God with all our heart, soul, strength and mind' (v 27) and a horizontal or social relationship with others – we are to 'love our neighbour as ourself' (v 27). Sometimes we put greater emphasis on one of these dimensions than the other. Those of us from an evangelical background have tended to place greater weight on the first, while those from the more liberal wing of the Church have tended to emphasise the second. It is essential that we get the right balance between them. E. Stanley Jones highlights this tension when he says, 'The personal without the social is a soul without a body. The social without the personal is body without a soul. The first is a ghost, the second is a corpse.'

People don't care how much we know
till they know how much we care.

Jesus demonstrated all aspects of this parable in the life he lived on earth. He related to people of different cultures from his own (Romans, Greeks), different economic status (rich and poor) and different physical condition (handicapped, lepers). He used his time, his resources and his abilities for the blessing of others. He showed us what love really is.

His final call to the expert in the law that day was, 'Go and do likewise' (Lk 10:37). It seems that the expert in the law was more interested in defining who his neighbour was, than being a neighbour. Jesus saw his motives and challenged him to the core.

This is the same challenge we face as congregations of Christians about to enter the twenty-first century. Do we continue to mouth nice statements among ourselves or from our pulpits about our oneness in Christ, or will we commit ourselves to the costly, sacrificial, God-honouring lifestyle of committed relationships? Will we take up the challenge of being the people that God has redeemed us to be, or will we sink to the relational standards of the world around us? Are we able to embrace the passion of Jesus and make it our own? How and when will the world take notice of the people of God?

As I have emphasised throughout this book, the central feature of Christianity is relationship. God has chosen this arena to demonstrate the uniqueness of his gospel to the world around. No other human programme, method, priority or substitute will suffice.

> *'The most widespread disease on this planet today is not cancer or AIDS, it is the feeling of being uncared for, unwanted – of being deserted and alone.'*
> **Mother Teresa**

Whatever else our congregations, small groups and leadership teams are known for, may we be known for the strength of our relationships together, to the glory of God.

IS OUR HELP REALLY HELPING?

Over the past 20 years or so there has been a great deal of discussion about the best ways aid agencies should be helping underprivileged people. Many development programmes funded and organised by the Western world to aid Third World countries have been found to be too imperialistic or paternalistic. Programmes may have helped people in the short term but the long-term results have tended to create dependency on the helping agency and locked people into poverty and despair. Finance has been controlled within the donor country often leaving the feeling that the Golden Rule has become, 'Those who have the gold, rule'.

We are facing situations in Western countries where we are increasingly having to help people in need not only within our congregations but also outside them. In our concern to help support those in need and the urgency of many situations, we must pause and seek to learn from the mistakes made in the past and not perpetuate these. We should learn from principles of operation that have been used successfully in partnership programmes where the 'haves' and the 'have-nots' have worked together to improve situations.

In the establishment of caring programmes, we need to work from underlying principles that are based on the values of the kingdom of God. Ultimately these values will reflect the nature of God and the way that he treats us as individuals.

Guiding principles

Preserve dignity:
When people are seen as a 'target group' or there is a weak–strong or donor–recipient relationship there are seeds present which may rob people of their dignity. It is difficult to receive help with dignity and nothing destroys a person's dignity quicker than dependency. We must guard against demean-

ing or condescending attitudes and work from attitudes of
equal-to-equal relationships. Wherever possible those who are
being helped should be encouraged to reciprocate by helping
others in return. Ways in which people being helped can earn,
work for or contribute to the support being given should be
explored.

The Old Testament principle of gleaning is instructive. God
asked those who had fields to leave handfuls of grain lying
on the ground or pockets at the edges of the fields unhar-
vested. This meant that the poor could come and be involved
in the harvesting process, thus maintaining a sense of dignity through their participation in the event.

Develop maturity:

God's intention for us his people is that we become mature in
Christ. This means we handle all areas of our life confidently,
that we are able to deal effectively with interpersonal relationships, that we understand our strengths and weaknesses and
accept who we are in Christ. Self-centredness is basically imma-
turity. It can be a major problem and we must always seek to get
to the root of the problem that we are dealing with in our own
or others' lives. For some this may be the irresponsible handling
of their finances. Here budgeting would encourage a more
mature attitude. For others it may mean help in simple food
preparation techniques to cut down on takeaways. It is not just
a better life that we are looking for but a way of living that we
need.
Note: A broken limb is supported in plaster only for as long as
it takes to become strong again. So should be our support to
those in need.

Share power:

The best help is given when people have an increasing control
over their own actions and destiny. The deacons in Acts 6 were
set up to make sure that the widows (Greek) were treated fair-
ly. The apostles (Jews) gathered the people together and elected
deacons, all of whom had Greek names. Obviously the apostles
shared power with the group that was being disadvantaged.
Sharing control gives those being helped a feeling of freedom –

one of humanity's cherished birthrights. Our care for others must mean our enabling of them to deal with their own needs. We also need to guard against the creation of power structures to catch the few miscreants. We must accept that those giving help will be 'ripped off' from time to time.

Encourage participation:

Many good programmes have been wrecked by the top–down approach. People need to participate in decision-making and in the development of their own programmes so as to feel that they 'own' the programme. They must be encouraged to act on their own needs and move towards wholeness. God permits his people to participate in reconciliation. We are allowed to shape our own history with him. It is very important that we release, encourage and draw on all of the enthusiasm and co-operation of those we are seeking to help in creation and support of ventures. For this to occur, trust between people will be essential. Unfortunately trust is easily violated but so hard to restore.

Decide on basics:

In the body of Christ some people will always have more, while others will have less. People are born with different abilities, and may have different opportunities to create resources. Jesus illustrated this when he told the parable of people who were given talents – ten, five and one. In both the nation of Israel and the early Church there was a wide diversity between the resources that people had. I do not believe that the Bible endorses the belief that everybody should own exactly the same resources, earn the same amount of money or have the same amount saved in the bank. What the Bible does encourage is that peoples' needs are met. In the early Church there was no needy person. The question is therefore, 'What are the essential needs of every human being?' The Bible indicates that these are adequate food, clothing and shelter. To this list we may also want to add access to education and medical care in our modern society.

Maintain confidentiality:

Both helper and helpee should maintain confidentiality in any transactions. This will help to preserve a person's dignity and avoid disparaging comparisons between those receiving help.

Recognise reciprocity:

No one is self-sufficient. Both the 'haves' and the 'have-nots' have much to learn from each other. Many people who have genuine financial need are more generous than those better off. They know what need feels like and have great compassion for others in similar positions. Poorer Christians can often teach those better off a lot about faith in God. They have had to learn to trust him in the practical everyday needs of living.

Co-ordinate effectively:

Sometimes, probably out of desperation, those in need seek to receive support from multiple outlets and play these off against each other. This does not ultimately help their cause but generates dishonesty and increases dependency. Therefore we need to establish sound guidelines in the areas of co-ordination. It is also very important not to raise people's expectations and then shatter them by poor or inefficient management procedures.

Guard relationships:

As with any area of human activity there is the high likelihood of relationships becoming tense or strained through misunderstanding. Also we will need to be patient with each other and apply liberal helpings of 1 Corinthians 13. Having pastoral people available to assist when relationships become tense is very important. I say 'when' rather than 'if', because anybody who has worked in the area dealing with matters affecting money or physical resources, will know how quickly misunderstandings and suspicion can occur here.

Receive with gratitude:

When we are on the receiving end of others' help we need to learn to receive graciously, with joy and with no feeling of obligation to repay the person who has helped us. For many of us this is difficult to do as we have been brought up to be so independent. Becoming a Christian frees me from the obligation of finding some way to repay those who help me. God does not ask us to repay to him what he gives to us, he simply asks us to learn to give to others.

Appendix II

Resources and Relationships – Some Suggestions

NOTE 1: These suggestions need to be worked out within the principles outlined in Appendix I.

NOTE 2: It is important that those who teach in congregations should understand and teach from a wider base, that of biblical economics, rather than just from the position of 'giving'.

Physical care through small groups
Can include a variety of forms of physical support, meals, firewood, monetary gifts, gardening, painting of homes for single parents, baby sitting, help when sick and so on.

Interest-free loans and gifts
Some congregations have established financial Trusts where money can be invested to help others with interest-free loans for such things as:
- Mortgages for homes
- Loans for the establishment of businesses or extension of businesses.
- Gifts/loans to purchase needs such as fridges, washing machines and food in genuine cases.
- Interest-free loans to service debts.
- Finance to provide transport – includes gifts and loans for those who genuinely need a vehicle.

It is important to have set procedures in place with such mechanisms as budgeting, automatic repayments and such like. This is to ensure that the root problem is addressed and money can be repaid. The repayments should be made at the level that the person can afford.

Monetary gifts
Such money comes from the congregation through special offer-

ings, general funds, earmarked giving and sponsorship for special events. It is gifted by a responsible body to those with genuine need.

Co-operative schemes
Food co-operatives where food is bought in bulk, may be subsidised by the congregation and then sold at reduced rates to those who may be struggling financially.

   Medical schemes where members of the congregation provide regular money for a fund and anybody who is part of the fund can have medical fees or prescription charges paid from this. This works on the basis that some who put into it will never draw on it as they can cover their own medical costs.

Christmas concern
Money from sponsorship to provide something special for needy families at Christmas.

Provide paid work
Those who have good incomes can be encouraged to provide paid work around their homes to those who have been unemployed or under-employed: lawns, gardens, house painting and housework. This is work that those who have good incomes would normally do themselves but provide it for others and in effect lower their standard of living by recompensing others for doing it for them.

Budgeting support
Getting to the root of financial problems is very important. Here budgeting pays an important role.

Simple nutritious meals
Courses for people to help them prepare cost-effective and nutritious meals for families.

Health needs
Simple preventative health care courses where ideas are presented that may save money on medical and prescription

expenses. Nurses within the congregation may be able to run these.

Youth involvement

A group of young people who are available for practical help in the community, or for people in the congregation on Saturday mornings. It is a very powerful testimony to the community for young people to be involved in such activities.

Sharing equipment

A good idea but very difficult to manage. People do not care for other people's equipment very well!

Food offering

A congregational service when families provide packaged food and children bring it to the front of the church as an offering. The food is directed to needy families.

Subsidised holidays

Holidays for single parents who often have no way of having a break. These paid for by the congregation, by sponsorship or by a trust.

Directory of trades and professions

This is helpful in a time of economic downturn. Encourages the congregation to support their own. Problem – Christians often think other Christians should do work for peanuts!

Support groups

Small groups of needy people who band together to support each other. Often leadership of these groups is a problem. Many needy people are so because they lack leadership skills and they often struggle to take initiative. An example of such a support group would be a group that arranged with a fruit farmer to gather fallen fruit together.

Swap meets

Where good quality clothes are gathered together and people can come and swap their own for what is available.

Special events

Sponsorship schemes whereby families can have special events subsidised, such as trips or meals in restaurants.

Appendix III

'One Anothers'
in the New Testament

'Be at peace with each other' (Mk 9:50).

'Wash one another's feet' (Jn 13:14).

'Love one another . . .' (Jn 13:34).

'Love one another' (Jn 13:35).

'Love each other . . .' (Jn 15:12).

'Love each other' (Jn 15:17).

'Be devoted to one another in brotherly love . . .' (Rom 12:10).

'Honour one another above yourselves' (Rom 12:10).

'Live in harmony with one another . . .' (Rom 12:16).

'Love one another . . .' (Rom 13:8).

'Stop passing judgment on one another' (Rom 14:13).

'Accept one another, then, just as Christ accepted you . . .' (Rom 15:7).

'Instruct one another' (Rom 15:14).

'Greet one another with a holy kiss . . .' (Rom 16:16).

'When you come together to eat, wait for each other' (1 Cor 11:33).

'Have equal concern for each other' (1 Cor 12:25).

'Greet one another with a holy kiss' (1 Cor 16:20).

'Greet one another with a holy kiss' (2 Cor 13:12).

'Serve one another in love' (Gal 5:13).

'If you keep on biting and devouring each other . . . you will be destroyed by each other' (Gal 5:15).

'Let us not become conceited, provoking and envying each other' (Gal 5:26).

'Carry each other's burdens . . .' (Gal 6:2).

'Be patient, bearing with one another in love' (Eph 4:2).

'Be kind and compassionate to one another . . .' (Eph 4:32).

'Forgiving each other . . .' (Eph 4:32).

'Speak to one another with psalms, hymns and spiritual songs'' (Eph 5:19).

'Submit to one another out of reverence for Christ' (Eph 5:21).

'In humility consider others better than yourselves' (Phil 2:3).

'Do not lie to each other' (Col 3:9).

'Bear with each other' (Col 3:13).

'Forgive whatever grievances you may have against one another' (Col 3:13).

'Teach . . . one another' (Col 3:16).

'Admonish one another' (Col 3:16).

'Make your love increase and overflow for each other' (1 Thess 3:12)

'Love each other' (1 Thess 4:9).

'Encourage each other . . .' (1 Thess 4:18).

'Encourage one another . . .' (1 Thess 5:11).

'Build each other up . . .' (1 Thess 5:11).

'Encourage one another daily . . .' (Heb 3:13).

'Spur one another on toward love and good deeds' (Heb 10:24).

'Encourage one another' (Heb 10:25).

'Do not slander one another' (Jas 4:11).

'Don't grumble against each other . . .' (Jas 5:9).

'Confess your sins to each other . . .' (Jas 5:16).

'Pray for each other' (Jas 5:16).

'Love one another deeply, from the heart' (1 Pet 1:22).

'Live in harmony with one another . . .'(1 Pet 3:8).

'Love each other deeply . . .' (1 Pet 4:8).

'Offer hospitality to one another without grumbling' (1 Pet 4:9).

'Each one should use whatever gift he has received to serve others . . .' (1 Pet 4:10).

'Clothe yourselves with humility toward one another' (1 Pet 5:5).

'Greet one another with a kiss of love' (1 Pet 5:14).

'Love one another' (1 Jn 3:11).

'Love one another . . .' (1 Jn 3:23).

'Love one another . . .' (1 Jn 4:7).

'Love one another . . .' (1 Jn 4:11).

'Love one another . . .' (1 Jn 4:12).

'Love one another. . . .' (2 Jn 5).

STUDY GUIDE

This study guide is designed for use in small groups. It is hoped that it will not only increase your understanding about the topic of relationships but also have practical implications in your life which will affect the vitality of your relationships with others.

Chapter 1: The Passion of Jesus

- Read John 17 together.
- Choose four instances where Jesus links himself and his Father to us and discuss together the implications of these instances, ie what have we been linked into?
- Chapter one gives a list of illustrations of the co-operative, united relationship of the Father, Son and Spirit (p 18). Can you think of other examples of this in Scripture?
- Ephesians 3:16–19 describes the unity of the Father, Son and Spirit in a Christian's life. Reflect on these verses together and discuss what this means to you practically. Maybe worship would be a fitting response.
- Reflect together on the list given in this chapter outlining something of the cost for Jesus to bring us restored relationships. Think of these instances in terms of today; events you have seen on TV or maybe experienced. Try to enter into what it cost Christ to make it possible for us to come back to God. Maybe worship would be a fitting response here too.
- Prayerfully reflect on your own relationships with other people. Try to feel the heart of Jesus for these. Pray together for a strengthening of these relationships.
- Discuss together the results of the unity of the Father with the Son:
  - authority (v 2)
  - insight (revelation) (v 6)
  - knowledge and faith (v 8)
  - protection and identity ('given a name') (v 11)
  - joy (v 13)
  - mission ('they were sent') (v 18)
  - set apart for God's special purpose (sanctification) (v 19)
  - unity and glory (v 21)

– witness (the world will know that the Father sent Christ and loves us) (v 23)

– revelation of the Father's love in us (v 26)

All of these are part of God's purposes for us in our unity with Christ. Select two or three and discuss together their implications for you personally and collectively.

• Pray that this passion of Jesus for unity will be birthed in you and other members of your small group or congregation.

Chapter 2: God's Priority: our Priority?

• The following is a paraphrase of Acts 2:42–47:

– v 42 They met constantly to hear teaching, to share their common life, to take part in the breaking of bread, and prayers.

– v 43 A deep sense of awe was upon them as God did marvellous things among them.

– v 44 All the believers continued together in close fellowship and shared their belongings with each other.

– v 45 Those who had plenty gave to those in need.

– v 46 With one desire they worshipped together regularly in their church and met for Communion in small groups in homes. They had meals together with unaffected joy and simplicity

– v 47 Praising God and enjoying the good will of all people. And God added daily to their group those whom he was saving.

Find all the sections (or words) in this part of Acts that talk about the relationships of those in this first church in Jerusalem. Discuss their significance for your congregation today.

• Read together 1 Corinthians 13. Wherever you come to the word 'love' put in your own name instead. When you finish you will have some idea of what God intends to do in your life. Prayerfully reflect on this when you have finished.

• The most often repeated command in the New Testament is to 'love one another'. Another word for 'love' is 'care'. List practical suggestions and plan together how you

might care better for each other in your small group. Think
of others in your congregation who might need some care
– plan to do this for them.

- The chart below lists references to the ministry of the Holy
  Spirit in our lives. Read together the verses in the third column and discuss how the relationships mentioned in these
  verses affect or are affected by the ministry of the Holy
  Spirit.

Reference	Ministry of the Holy Spirit	Relationship context
Galatians 5:18	The leading of the Spirit	Galatians 5:13-26
Ephesians 4:30	Grieving the Spirit	Ephesians 4:25-32
Ephesians 5:18	The filling of the Spirit	Ephesians 5:1-21

Chapter 3: Keep it up – Sort it out!

- Read Romans 12:3–21 together. Identify the relationship
  statements in these verses and discuss how you could 'put
  feet on these' in working them out practically among yourselves and others in your congregation.
- The New Testament says that we should not judge each
  other (Rom 14:13). However it also says that we should
  judge others in disputes (1 Cor 6:5). In these references the
  Greek words give two different meanings for the word
  'judge'. The first means to pass judgment or to condemn,
  while the second means to discriminate or discern. Discuss
  how and when we should (or should not) be judging
  others.
- Galatians 6:2 says we should carry each other's burdens
  but verse 5 says we should carry our own burden. The first
  Greek word for load means crushing burden while the second means 'knapsack'. Discuss together what the differences may be in everyday living. When should you help
  carry another person's load?
- Hospitality is encouraged in the New Testament (1 Pet 4:9,
  Rom 12:13). Plan ways that you could do more of this.
  How could you involve people that you are not so close to?
  What about lonely people in your congregation? What
  ways can hospitality be shown if you do not own your own
  home? Remember it is not sufficient to just talk about these

things, we need to do them.
- Develop an accountable relationship with someone. Apply the suggestions made in this chapter.

Chapter 4: Let's Party

- List ways in which you can honour each other and then decide individually what you will do within the next few days to honour another person.
- Go around the group and share the things that you appreciate about each other.
- Discuss why it is we so often find it hard to forgive other people. If you are struggling with forgiving someone right now, ask the group to pray for you and maybe suggest ways that you can overcome this.
  Note: Sometimes it may not be appropriate to tell others what it is you are struggling with.
- Recently a congregation made the following suggestions as to how they could encourage each other;
  - telling people you are praying for them
  - hugs
  - listening carefully
  - giving an unexpected gift
  - sharing a verse
  - sending a letter
  - sending a card
  - making a phone call
  - giving a compliment
  - giving some baking
  - sending flowers
  - being patient in a difficult situation
  - helping around the home in practical ways
  - giving a meal
  - providing hospitality
  - waving to someone
  - giving an invitation for another person to visit your home
  - saying thanks
  - giving a helping hand
  - supporting someone through a difficulty
  - doing the dishes

- giving thanks for everyday things
- sharing something about your own life
- giving praise
- bringing a prophetic word
- making an apology
- giving a smile
- asking forgiveness
- sharing Christian books
- heeding another's advice
- sending a letter of thanks
- placing a hand on a shoulder
- giving and receiving good news
- remembering birthdays and other significant occasions

- Maybe you could list some more and then individually decide who you will encourage within the next few days and how you will do it.
- Divide your group into pairs and each member of the pair talk about themselves to the other for two minutes. The other partner then tries to repeat what they have been told. Talk about the importance of listening carefully – with eyes and ears.
- Discuss ways in which people have encouraged you, give examples of this.
- Discuss ways in which you can show acceptance of a person who is doing things or living in a way that you disagree with.
- How can we provoke one another to love (Heb 10:24)?
- Place all the names of people in your group in a hat and each pull one out. Make sure it is not your own. Become an angel and do something anonymously for that person before the group meets again. At your next meeting each person tells the group what their anonymous angel did for them. Continue to keep the angels anonymous.

Chapter 5: I'll do it my Way

- Read through the set of questions at the beginning of the chapter (p 69) and then discuss together how you react in those situations.
- Together list illustrations of individualism that can be seen

in today's society.
- Between now and next time your group meets, watch the TV news and note some of the things spoken about in 2 Timothy 3:1–4. Compare your notes next time you meet.
- We often focus on rights. Discuss what your responsibilities are in the following situations;
  - This group
  - Your family
  - Your congregation
  - Your community
  - Your country

Chapter 6: Being Number One
- On a scale of 1–10 estimate how competitive you feel you are. Now get a close friend to make their estimate of your competitiveness, while you do it for them. Discuss these results together.
- Discuss ways in which competitiveness can help us and how it hinders us.
- Each member of the group is to identify areas in their lives where they need to be less competitive. Go around the group and encourage each member to share one area with the rest of the group. Pray for each other about these areas.

Chapter 7: Shot in the Foot
- Discuss together the implication of this chapter for your small group or your congregation.
- Think of people you know well. List their strengths, abilities and gifts. Now think of their weaknesses. Do you tend to dismiss what they are or do because of their weaknesses? Pray for them.
- If you are part of a team, discuss the implications of this chapter for your team.

Chapter 8: Solutions are Humbling
The crucial thing about this study is not what happens in our heads but what we do with it in our hearts.
- Reflect on the list of statements about humility which commence 'Biblical humility means' and then discuss them together (p 107). Think of some others ways that you can

describe humility.

- Discuss the difficulties you have in seeking to be genuinely humble. Pray for each other in this area.
- Read and study together Romans 6:1–23 (cross) and 8:1–17 (Spirit). Pray that you will be able to apply these to your life.
- Discuss the paradox that the monk gave to his students (p 116). Read what Jesus said about this in John 12:25. What does this mean for us today?
- If there is somebody who particularly irritates you, or opposes you? Then pray God's blessing on that person each day for a week.
- Discuss together situations where you have been misunderstood. How did it happen and what was done about it?
- If you are struggling in areas which this chapter covers, share this with someone you have confidence in. Seek their counsel and prayerful oversight of your life as you work through this.

Chapter 9: Resources and Relationships
Warning: This is a controversial topic. Expect strong reactions from people. Answers will not always be easy or clear cut.

- Read Luke 16:1–15 and discuss the following questions together.
  - How can we use worldly wealth to gain friends? (v 9)
  - What does it mean – 'welcome us into eternal dwellings?' (v 9)
  - What do you think the 'little' refers to that Jesus talks about in verse 10? What would be the 'much'?
  - In what ways are we untrustworthy with worldly wealth? (v11)
  - How do we serve money? (v 13)
  - What would be the characteristics of a 'lover of money'? (v 14)
  - In the following verses, what are the implications about being 'lovers of money'? (1 Tim 3:3, 1 Tim 6:10, 2 Tim 3:4, Heb 13:5, 1 Pet 5:2)
- How can you put 1 John 3:16–18 into action in your congregation?

- What would be the qualities of a good steward? How do we apply this to the way we handle our resources?
- Read the following verses in Deuteronomy and discuss together the questions.
  - Deuteronomy 8:18. In what ways does God give people the ability to produce wealth?
  - Deuteronomy 14:28–29. We cannot carry out in practice what this verse describes, but what is the principle that we need to follow?
  - Deuteronomy 16:17. How can we put into practice the principle outlined in this verse?
- Discuss some of the suggestions in Appendix II. Can your group implement any of these?

Chapter 10: Doing it Better

Although this chapter is written from the point of view of a congregation many of the ideas can be implemented by small groups.

- Look through the list of suggestions mentioned in the chapter as to ways to enhance relationships and try some of them in your group.

Chapter 11: Teams are in

The following ideas are best used in teams but can be applied to small groups. The team leader will need to decide if the team is ready for such an exercise and will need to be particularly sensitive to members of the team who have a low or unhealthy self-image.

This exercise is best done when you have plenty of time, maybe at a weekend retreat.

Prepare the chart below and give a copy to each person in the team. The names are the names of the team members. Get each of them to fill it out before you meet together.

- Select up to four key words or thoughts relating to each team member and yourself. Three of these will affirm areas of strength (ability, gifting) that you perceive in them. The fourth will indicate one area in which you would like to see growth and development in that team member. In the

column under 'Own Name' fill in the appropriate words for

	Own Name	Name 1	Name 2	Name 3	Name 4	etc
Name 1						
Own Name						
Name 3						
Name 4						
Name 5						
etc						

  yourself and also for each other person listed on the sheet.
- Get all members of the team to do the same. When this stage is finished each team member should have one *column* completed.
- Now go around the group and get each person to read out the words he or she has selected for each of the team members, including him or herself. Each team member records these key words in the *column* under the name of the person reading out the words. When this stage is finished each team member should have filled in the complete grid.
- Now look across the *row* bearing your name and identify the recurring words or ideas that convey what the other team members see as your strengths (abilities, giftings). Discuss these among yourselves. Remember – gratitude, rather than pride, is an appropriate response to our strengths. How does each team member feel about what others perceive as their strengths? Express these feelings to each other.
- In the light of each team member's strengths, is he or she fulfilling the appropriate role within the team or ministry that the team oversees? If not this may need to be adjusted.
- Be sensitive to one another as you discuss the areas that need growth and development.
- Now take every member of the team one at a time and focus on their strengths, affirm these, pray for them, lay hands on them, bring encouragement, maybe bring a prophetic word to them.
- Also pray about the areas needing growth and development. You could make practical suggestions to each other as to how these areas could be developed.

- Consider giving one another permission to speak into each other's lives.
- Other helpful exercises that can be done as a team include
  a) Discover your motivational gifts (as found in Romans 12:6–8). Christian bookshops may have the book *Discover your God-given Gifts*, by Don and Katie Fortune (published by Chosen Books).
  b) Myers-Briggs materials can also be quite useful.

Chapter 12: The Awesome Power of Words

Get someone in the group to read out Martin Luther King's 'I have a dream' speech below. If you can watch it on video or computer CD disc, or hear it audio tape, all the better.

I say to you today, even though we face the difficulties of today and tomorrow, I still have a dream. It is a dream that is deeply rooted in the American dream. I have a dream that one day this nation will rise up, live out the true meaning of its creed. We hold these truths to be self evident, that all men are created equal.

I have a dream that one day on the red hills of Georgia the sons of former slaves and the sons of former slave-owners will be able to sit down together at the table of brotherhood. I have a dream that one day even the state of Mississippi, a state sweltering with the heat of oppression, will be transformed into an oasis of freedom and justice.

I have a dream that my four little children one day will live in a nation where they will not be judged by the colour of their skin, but by the content of their character. I have a dream that one day every valley shall be exalted, every hill and mountain shall be made low. The rough places will be made plain and the crooked places will be made straight. This is the faith that I go back to the South with. With this faith we will be able to hew out of the mountains of despair the stone of hope. With this faith we will be able to work together, to pray together, to struggle together, to go to jail together, to stand up for freedom together, knowing that one day we will be free. This will be the day when all of God's children will be able to sing with new meaning, 'Let Freedom ring.'

So let freedom ring from the prodigious hilltops of New Hampshire; let freedom ring from the mighty mountains of New York. But not only that. Let freedom ring from Stone Mountain of Georgia. Let freedom ring from every hill and molehill of Mississippi, from every mountainside.

When we allow freedom to ring from every town and every hamlet, from every state and every city, we will be able to speed up that day when all of God's children, black men and white men, Jews and Gentiles, Protestants and Catholics, will be able to join hands and sing in the words of the old Negro spiritual, 'Free at last! Free at last! Great God Almighty, we are free at last!'

Discuss together the power of words as seen in this speech.

- Does the group agree that things we say can never be neutral, they must either be helpful or unhelpful? Consider Figure 5 showing creative and destructive words (p 170) and try to think of anything that we may say which is neutral.
- Make sure each person has a copy of the 'wise words about words' (the references from Proverbs) and ask group members to select three statements which particularly appeal to them and say why this is so.
- The group leader prepares a statement with about 7 to 8 facts in it. Use the example below as a model but create your own.

    I want you to go to_____ (name a local shop) and buy me a dozen red apples and a kilo of pears. Please bring these to my home by 3 pm today. If I am out, leave them on the back doorstep and I will pay you by cheque when I next see you.

    The leader whispers this statement in the ear of the first person who then whispers in the ear of the next and so on around the group. The last person to receive the message then tells the rest of the group aloud what they received. The leader then compares this last message with the first. Discuss the implication of this for us in terms of passing on and accepting at face value things that are told to us.

Chapter 13: A Parable for our Time

- Discuss ways in which we should be sensitive to those of other cultures.
- Discuss ways in which you could build friendships with those of other cultures
- Are there any people living near you who would be equivalent to the man in the parable who was found lying on the road? Is there anything you or your group can do to help such people?
- Make a week's evaluation of your time. Account for every 15 minutes. At the end of the week carefully analyse how you spent the week. Answer the following questions:
  - How much time was spent on essential activities such as eating, sleeping, washing etc?
  - How much time was spent in work?
  - How much time was in relaxation? Watching TV? Reading? Socialising? Other?
  - How much time, outside of work, was spent attending to the needs of others?
  - List other activities?
  - There are 168 hours in a week. How much time can you not account for?
  - Work out percentages. Do you need to make some adjustments?
- If you need help to use your time more effectively approach someone for help.
- Discuss together your natural talents, acquired skills and spiritual gifts. In what ways could these be better used to help others.

NOTES

Introduction
1. Throughout this book the author will normally use the word 'congregation' to describe the people and/or activities of a group of Christians in a local church.
2. 'Pointers', Bulletin of the Christian Research Association, March 1994, Vol. 4:1. Rowland Croucher.
3. Brian Hathaway, *Beyond Renewal – the Kingdom of God* (Milton Keynes: Word, 1990).

Chapter 2
1. Not his real name.
2. His wife. Not her real name.
3. See list in Appendix III.
4. Jn 13:34(2x), 13:35, 15:12, 15:17, Rom 12:10, 13:8, 1 Thess 3:12, 4:9, 1 Pt 1:22, 4:8, 1 Jn 3:11, 3:23, 4:7, 4:11, 4:12, 2 Jn 5.

Chapter 3
1. Some examples include Rom 12:3–21, 1 Cor 13, Gal 5:13–26, Eph 4:1–7, 22–32.

Chapter 4
1. E Stanley Jones. *The Unshakable Kingdom and the Unchanging Person* (London: Abingdon Press, 1972).
2. Not her real name.
3. Robert D. Lupton, *For Theirs is the Kingdom* (London: Harper and Row, 1989) pp 98–100.

Chapter 5
1. My friend, not his real name.
2. Wife of newly married couple, not her real name.

Chapter 6
1. Trina Paulia, *Hope for the Flowers* (Mahwah. N.J.: Paulist Press, 1978) pp 21–94.
2. Andrew Murray, source unknown.

Chapter 8
1. See Chapter 1.
2. Some well known examples include: 2 Chron 7:14, Prov 22:4, Is 57:15, Mic 6:8, Matt 23:12, Col 3:12, Eph 4:2.
3. Not their real names.

Chapter 9
1. Further references where the root *koinon* is linked to finances and resources: Lk 5:10, Act 4:32, Rom 15:27, Phil 4:14, 4:15, Heb 13:16.
2. E Stanley Jones, *The Unshakable Kingdom and the Unchanging Person* (London: Abingdon Press, 1972) p 116.
3. For further discussion on Biblical Economics see 'The Oxford Declaration on Christian Faith and Economics', *Transformation,* Vol. 7 No. 2, April/June 1990.

Chapter 10
1. Not his real name.

Chapter 11
1. See Chapter 8.
2. See Acts 2:42, 4:35–37, 6:6, 9:27, 15:2, 4, 6, 22, 23, 33.
3. Quote attributed to Winston Churchill.
4. Further practical suggestions for the recognition of gifting and abilities are made in the Study Guide for this chapter on p 202.

Chapter 12
1. These are taken from the Living Bible.